PHOTOS BY RETO GUNTLI · TEXT BY SUNIL SETHI
ED. ANGELIKA TASCHEN

INSIDE ASIA

TASCHEN

HONG KONG KÖLN LONDON LOS ANGELES MADRID PARIS TOKYO

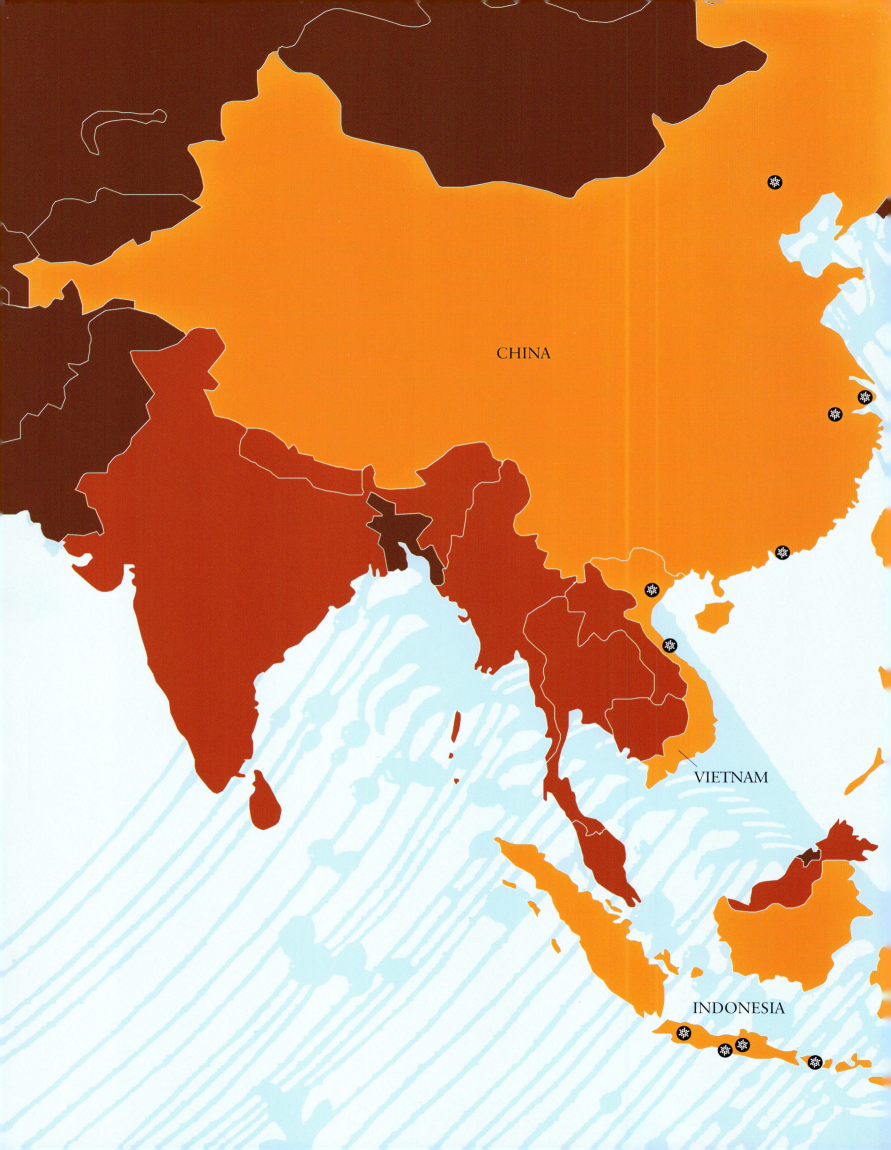

CHINA

VIETNAM

INDONESIA

JAPAN

PHILIPPINES

An Old Java House

The Shrimp House

Losari Coffee Plantation

Linda Garland

Amanjiwo

Cipicong

John and Cynthia Hardy

Begawan Giri Estate

Aulia's House

Carolina Tety

A House In Seminyak

Anneke's Guesthouse

Anneke van Waesberghe

Taman Bebek

Taman Selini

Amanjiwo
Java

In the shadow of 500 Buddhas, a temple to nurture body and soul.

In ancient Buddhist and Hindu scripture, *rasa* means the "essence of life": an intuitive but powerful sense of radiance and insight. Nowhere is such a feeling more lucid than in the eighth-century Buddhist sanctuary of Borobudur, the largest in the world.

More than 500 Buddhas, hewn from the local limestone, rise out of the rice fields of the Kedu Plain. Volcanic peaks punctuate the horizon; directly beyond Borobudur is the hill of Tidar, known in legend as the very head of the nail that pins Java to the earth. In a landscape of such evolved harmony is a resort inspired by the architecture of Borobudur. *Amanjiwo* means "peaceful soul". At its heart is a monolith with a soaring bell-shaped rotunda. Motifs of circles, squares and crescents echo patterns of ancient temples; high walls thick with spider lilies and morning glory shade the rooms; stone walkways link the suites to the main building and pool. But Amanjiwo's pilot star is Borobudur – unveiled at dawn through the vanishing mist – and just a brief ride away, on horse-cart or a bicycle.

In alten buddhistischen und hinduistischen Schriften bedeutet das Wort *rasa* »Inbegriff des Lebens«. Damit ist ein intuitives Gefühl von Erleuchtung und Verständnis gemeint. Nirgends kann man rasa intensiver spüren als in dem buddhistischen Tempel Borobodur aus dem 8. Jahrhundert, dem größten Tempel der Welt.

Über 500 Buddhas aus Kalkstein ragen aus den Reisfeldern der Keduebene. Vulkangipfel ragen in den Himmel, und direkt hinter dem Borobodur liegt der Hügel Tidar – der Legende nach der Kopf des Nagels, der Java in der Erde hält. Die Hotelanlage ist von der Architektur des Borobodur inspiriert. Amanjiwo bedeutet »Seelenfrieden«. In der Mitte steht ein Monolith mit einer aufragenden glockenförmigen Rotunde. Die dekorativen Kreise, Vierecke und Halbmonde wirken wie ein Echo auf Muster der alten Tempel. Hohe bepflanzte Mauern geben den Räumen Schatten. Kieswege verbinden die Suiten mit dem Hauptgebäude und dem Swimmingpool. Die Hauptattraktion von Amanjiwo bleibt jedoch der Borobodur, der morgens durch den aufsteigenden Nebel sichtbar wird und nur eine kurze Kutschfahrt oder eine Spritztour mit dem Fahrrad entfernt liegt.

Dans les textes sacrés bouddhiques et hindouistes, *rasa* signifie «l'essence de la vie», sentiment intuitif mais puissant d'illumination et de compréhension. Nulle part le rasa n'est aussi manifeste qu'au sanctuaire de Borobudur datant du 8e siècle, le plus grand sanctuaire bouddhique au monde.

Plus de 500 bouddhas taillés dans le calcaire local surgissent des rizières de la plaine de Kedu, sur l'arrière-plan de volcans. Directement derrière Borobudur s'élève la colline de Tidar, qui, selon la légende, serait la tête du clou qui attache Java à la terre. C'est dans ce paysage harmonieux que se trouve le complexe hôtelier d'Amanjiwo, «l'âme en paix», inspiré par l'architecture de Borobudur. En son centre se dresse un monolithe duquel surgit une rotonde en forme de cloche. Les cercles, carrés et croissants sont des motifs empruntés à l'architecture sacrée traditionnelle. De hauts murs couverts de lys araignées et de belles-de-jour donnent de l'ombre ; des chemins dallés de pierre relient les suites au bâtiment central et à la piscine. Mais l'attraction d'Amanjiwo est Borobudur – qui se dévoile à l'aube lorsque la brume se dissipe –, à deux pas en carriole ou en bicyclette.

Cipicong
Java

Venice rises in the East.

A learned European friend who once visited Cipicong (pronounced Chippy-chong), Jaya Ibrahim's homage to his Javanese roots, came back gasping: "It is like Venice rising in the East". As the crescent moon rises over the lush rice bowl in the shadow of Mount Salak, Cipicong acquires an operatic dimension, with no boundaries or fencing, just an infinity of surrounding hills and valleys.

An hour and a half's drive south of Jakarta, Cipicong is sited near a palace where Raffles, and later the Dutch and Soekarno, lived. Ibrahim, who worked in London for many years before returning home, built a house with many references – a Venetian window, colonnaded verandas, Palladian arches – but resolved the styles into a seamless synthesis. The details are quintessentially Eastern: banana leaves replace acanthus leaves in the decorative capitals and jasmine buds, borrowed from a tenth-century Javanese palace, crown the loggia. Like many creative artists, Jaya Ibrahim carries numerous styles in his head. In Cipicong he has triumphantly reinterpreted them to create something uniquely his own.

Als ein gebildeter Europäer in Cipicong (»tschippitschong« ausgesprochen) – Jaya Ibrahims Hommage an seine javanischen Wurzeln – zu Besuch war, staunte er: »Als ginge Venedig im Osten auf!« Wenn die Mondsichel über den üppigen Reisfeldern im Schatten des Berges Salak aufgeht, verleiht sie Cipicong etwas Opernhaftes, Grenzenloses in einer Unendlichkeit von Hügeln und Tälern.

Cipicong ist von Jakarta aus mit dem Auto in anderthalb Stunden zu erreichen und liegt in der Nähe eines Palastes, in dem die britische Kolonialbeamte Raffles, später die Holländer und Indonesiens erster Staatspräsident Sukarno wohnten. Ibrahim, der vor seiner Rückkehr in die Heimat lange in London arbeitete, hat sich ein Haus voller Anspielungen gebaut – hier ein venezianisches Fenster, dort säulengeschmückte Veranden, Bögen wie bei Palladio, aber es ist ihm gelungen, die verschiedenen Stile zu einer vollkommenen Synthese zu führen. Im Detail ist alles grundsätzlich östlich: Bananenblätter statt Akanthus zieren die Kapitelle, Jasminknospen die Loggia. Wie viele andere Künstler lässt sich auch Jaya Ibrahim von den verschiedensten Stilrichtungen inspirieren, die er in Cipicong neu interpretiert und zu einer gelungenen Eigenkreation zusammengefügt hat.

Un éminent confrère européen qui s'était un jour rendu à Cipicong (à prononcer «tchipitchong»), l'hommage rendu par Jaya Ibrahim à ses racines javanaises, a déclaré à son retour, ravi : «C'est la Venise de l'Orient!» Lorsque le croissant de lune s'élève au-dessus des luxuriantes rizières à l'ombre du mont Salak, Cipicong atteint une dimension lyrique : ni limites ni clôtures, juste des collines et vallées à perte de vue.

A une heure et demie de route de Jakarta, Cipicong est situé à proximité du palais dans lequel ont vécu Raffles et, plus tard, les Hollandais et Sukarno. Ibrahim, qui a travaillé de longues années à Londres, s'est construit une maison aux références nombreuses – fenêtre vénitienne, vérandas à péristyle, arcs palladiens –, tout en fondant ces styles en une synthèse parfaite. Les détails sont par essence orientaux : des feuilles de bananier remplacent les feuilles d'acanthe dans les chapiteaux et des boutons de jasmin, motif emprunté à un palais javanais du 10e siècle, surmontent la loggia. Comme bien d'autres artistes, Jaya Ibrahim s'est frotté à de nombreux styles. Cipicong en est une brillante réinterprétation toute personnelle.

✻ **PREVIOUS PAGES** The fountain in the colonnaded courtyard is a 14th-century urn. Eighty-four terracotta pots are arranged around it, lit with candles on special occasions. **FACING PAGE** The view from the study through the Venetian window faces east. The patterned concrete floors are from designs of old Javanese batiks. **ABOVE** The eastern façade with the Venetian window, crowned by lotus buds. ✻ **VORHERGEHENDE DOPPELSEITE** Der Brunnen in dem säulengeschmückten Hof plätschert in einer Urne aus dem 14. Jahrhundert. In den vierundachtzig Terrakottatöpfen werden zu besonderen Anlässen Kerzen angezündet. **LINKE SEITE** Blick nach Osten aus dem Fenster im Arbeitszimmer. Das Muster der Betonböden ist alter javanischer Batik entnommen. **OBEN** Die östliche Fassade mit dem von Lotusknospen gekrönten venezianischen Fenstern. ✻ **DOUBLE PAGE PRECEDENTE** Cette fontaine de la cour à colonnade est une urne du 14e siècle. Dans les 84 pots en terre cuite, on allume des bougies en des occasions particulières. **PAGE DE GAUCHE** La fenêtre vénitienne du bureau donne à l'est. **CI-DESSOUS** Les motifs des sols en béton sont empruntés à des batiks javanais anciens. **CI-DESSUS** La fenêtre vénitienne est surmontée de boutons de lotus.

※ **PREVIOUS PAGES** A huge daybed, resting on concrete feet, was inspired by a throne on a bas-relief at Borobudur. The polished concrete steps lead to the *pendopo*, the traditional receiving area. **ABOVE** Meals are often taken on the veranda. **FACING PAGE** Old cabinets, jars and lacquer ware line the kitchen flooded with light. ※ **VORHERGEHENDE DOPPELSEITE** Das große Ruhebett ruht auf Betonfüßen und wurde nach dem Bild eines Throns auf einem Basrelief des Borobodur entworfen. Die Stufen aus poliertem Beton führen zum *pendopo*, dem traditionellen Empfangsbereich. **OBEN** Die Mahlzeiten werden häufig im Freien serviert. **RECHTE SEITE** alte Schränke, Gefäße und Lackutensilien in der lichtdurchfluteten Küche. ※ **DOUBLE PAGE PRECEDENTE** Ce grand lit de repos est inspiré d'un trône représenté sur un bas-relief de Borobudur. Les marches de béton poli mènent au *pendopo*, la zone de réception traditionnelle. **CI-DESSUS** On prend souvent les repas sur la véranda. **PAGE DE DROITE** Meubles de rangement anciens, pots et objets en laque tapissent les murs de la cuisine légèrement encombrée.

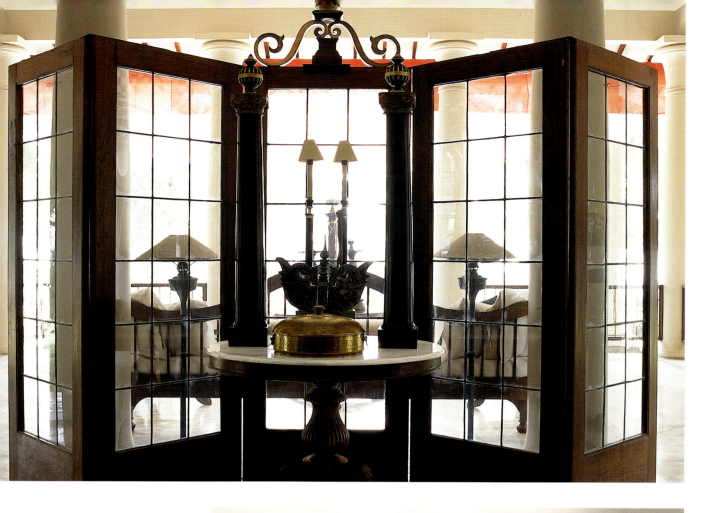

✳ **FACING PAGE** The five-leaf screen between the veranda and dining room was created from discarded old doors. A pair of rattan chairs designed by Jaya Ibrahim flank a door leading to a bedroom. **ABOVE** A mirror from Sumatra and a pair of 18th-century doors form the headboard of the bed. The cut crystal hanging lamp is also from Sumatra. **FOLLOWING PAGES** looking from the house towards the daybed. The square platform is for Javanese dance performances. ✳ **LINKE SEITE** Der fünfflügelige Raumteiler zwischen der Veranda und dem Speisesaal wurde aus ausrangierten alten Türen gebaut. Die beiden von Jaya Ibrahim entworfenen Rattanstühle stehen neben einer Tür, die zu einem der Schlafzimmer führt. **OBEN** Das Kopfteil des Bettes besteht aus einem Spiegel aus Sumatra und zwei Türen aus dem 18. Jahrhundert. Die Lampe aus geschliffenem Kristallglas stammt ebenfalls aus Sumatra. **FOLGENDE DOPPELSEITE** Blick vom Haus zum Ruhebett. Auf der viereckigen Fläche werden häufig javanische Tänze vorgeführt. ✳ **PAGE DE GAUCHE** Le paravent à cinq panneaux séparant la véranda de la salle à manger a été réalisé à partir de portes anciennes mises au rebut. Deux chaises en rotin signées Jaya Ibrahim flanquent la porte de la chambre. **CI-DESSUS** Un miroir de Sumatra et deux portes du 18ᵉ siècle servent de tête de lit. Le lustre en cristal taillé est aussi de Sumatra. **DOUBLE PAGE SUIVANTE** le lit de repos vu de la maison. L'estrade au premier plan est utilisée pour des spectacles de danses traditionnelles.

LOSARI
COFFEE PLANTATION
Java

Freshly picked and roasted,
the aroma of coffee melts into volcanic mists.

In 1992, Gabriella Teggia, an indefatigable Italian who has lived in Indonesia for many years, was hiking in the highlands of central Java when she came across an early 19th-century mansion in a state of utter disrepair.

Set in a 60-acre plantation, it had been home to generations of Dutch coffee planters; later the estate was gifted to a hero of Indonesia's independence. Teggia bought the Losari plantation from his widow and embarked on a major restoration with the Italian architect Andrea Magnaghi. Today, Losari is an exclusive resort and spa but visitors are encouraged to treat it as home away from home. Surrounded by eight volcanic peaks – of which Mount Merapi is still active – the area is full of wonderful hikes and trips to old Hindu temples. The main house, overlooking verandas and replanted gardens, has been converted into library and music room. And the estate still produces 30 tons of organically-grown Robusta coffee, which is sun dried, handpicked and roasted in the traditional way.

1992 wanderte die unermüdliche Italienerin Gabriella Teggia, die seit vielen Jahren in Indonesien lebt, durch die Hochebenen Zentral-Javas, als sie inmitten einer 30 Hektar großen Plantage ein Herrenhaus aus dem 19. Jahrhundert entdeckte.

Die Villa, in der Generationen von holländischen Kaffeepflanzern gelebt hatten und die später einem Helden der indonesischen Unabhängigkeitsbewegung zugesprochen worden war, befand sich in einem schlimmen Zustand. Teggia kaufte sie der Witwe des Helden ab und begann, sie mithilfe des italienischen Architekten Andrea Magnaghi zu renovieren. Inzwischen ist aus Losari ein exklusives Wellness-Resort geworden, in dem sich die Gäste trotz aller Eleganz wie zu Hause fühlen können. Die vulkanreiche Gegend lädt zu Ausflügen zu alten Hindu-Tempeln ebenso ein wie zum Wandern. Das Haupthaus mit Blick über Veranden und neu bepflanzte Gartenanlagen beherbergt heute die Bibliothek und ein Musikzimmer. Die eigentliche Plantage produziert immer noch 30 Tonnen Bio-Robusta-Kaffee, der in der Sonne getrocknet, handverlesen und auf traditionelle Art geröstet wird.

En 1992, Gabriella Teggia, une Italienne infatigable qui vit en Indonésie depuis longtemps, faisait de la randonnée sur les hauts plateaux de Java-Centre, lorsqu'elle est tombée sur une villa du 19e siècle complètement délabrée.

Située dans une plantation de 30 hectares, elle avait été la demeure de générations de planteurs de café, avant d'être donnée en récompense à un héros de l'indépendance nationale. Gabriella Teggia a racheté l'exploitation à la veuve de ce dernier et s'est lancée dans une restauration en profondeur avec le concours de l'architecte italien Andrea Magnaghi. Losari est désormais un centre de remise en forme exclusif, et son élégance n'intimide pas les clients qui s'y sentent chez eux. Dans cette région de volcans, on peut faire de superbes randonnées et visiter des temples hindouistes anciens. La maison principale, qui donne sur des vérandas et des jardins replantés, a été convertie en bibliothèque et salle de musique. La propriété produit encore chaque année 30 tonnes de café robusta biologique, séché au soleil, trié à la main et torréfié de manière traditionnelle.

✻ **PREVIOUS PAGES** The days at Losari are spent on deep verandas, sipping home-grown fresh coffee on Art-Deco style chairs. **ABOVE** View from a wall of carved Javanese panels into a bedroom suite at Losari. **RIGHT** A sunken bath in a suite adds to Losari's period atmosphere. **FACING PAGE** An old bed from Madura embellished with cotton drapes and cushions is transformed into a daytime divan. ✻ **VORHERGEHENDE DOPPELSEITEN** Auf Losari verbringt man seine Tage auf großen Veranden und genießt den hier angebauten Kaffee auf Art-Déco-Stühlen. **OBEN** Blick von einer Wand mit javanischer Holzvertäfelung in das Schlafzimmer einer Suite in Losari **RECHTS** Die versenkte Badewanne trägt zu der historischen Atmosphäre dieser Suite bei. **RECHTE SEITE** Ein altes Bett aus Madura mit hübschen Vorhängen und Kissen aus Baumwolle verwandelt sich tagsüber in einen Diwan ✻ **DOUBLES PAGES PRECEDENTES** A Losari, on passe ses journées sur de grandes vérandas, à siroter du café dans des fauteuils coloniaux Art Déco. **CI-DESSUS** Ce claustra javanais en bois dévoile l'intérieur d'une suite. **A DROITE** une baignoire encastrée dans une suite ajoute au charme suranné de Losari. **PAGE DE DROITE** Agrémenté de tentures de coton et de coussins, ce lit ancien provenant de Madura fait un agréable lit de repos.

✳ **FACING PAGE** the master bedroom in a Losari suite. Traditional Javanese fare. **ABOVE** a bedroom under sloping rafters, furnished with colonial style furniture. ✳ **LINKE SEITE** ein Schlafzimmer im Kolonialstil. Traditionelles javanisches Geschirr. **OBEN** das große Schlafzimmer in einer Suite auf Losari, mit schrägem Dach. ✳ **PAGE DE GAUCHE** une chambre mansardée meublée en style colonial. Un repas javanais traditionnnel. **CI-DESSSUS** la chambre principale d'une suite.

※ **ABOVE** Coffee beans are ground on the plantation in a traditional mill. **FACING PAGE** Sunset views overlooking volcanic peaks from a private balcony. ※ **OBEN** Auf der Plantage werden die Kaffeebohnen mithilfe einer traditionellen Kaffeemühle gemahlen. **RECHTE SEITE** Blick vom Balkon auf die Vulkangipfel in der Abenddämmerung. ※ **CI-DESSUS** La plantation utilise un moulin a café traditionnel. **PAGE DE DROITE** Vu du balcon, le coucher du soleil sur les pics volcaniques.

※ **ABOVE** Coffee beans are cleaned, sorted and ground at Losari in the traditional way. ※ **OBEN** Die Kaffeebohnen werden auf traditionelle Weise gesäubert, sortiert und gemahlen. ※ **CI-DESSUS** A Losari, les grains de café sont nettoyés, triés et moulus selon la tradition.

※ **ABOVE** 30 tons of coffee are organically grown at Losari. It is handpicked and stored for sun drying in jute sacks. ※ **OBEN** 30 Tonnen Bio-Kaffee werden jährlich auf Losari angebaut. Die Bohnen werden handverlesen und zum Trocknen in Jutesäcken in die Sonne gestellt. ※ **CI-DESSUS** 30 tonnes de café bio sont produites chaque année à Losari. Le café est ramassé à la main et mis à sécher au soleil dans des sacs de jute.

Begawan Giri Estate

UBUD Bali

"Sublime" is the favoured verdict on a retreat for the rich and famous.

Begawan Giri Estate is an enclave so quiet and exclusive that its starred guest list is just a vague rumour. Donna Karan, Susan Sarandon and Sting are said to have stayed here.

An English entrepreneur, Bradley Gardner, with a long association with Southeast Asia, found the superb site above a valley bound by two rivers to build a vacation home. Together with his wife Debbie, he gradually planted 2,500 trees on the hillside and created a water garden down by the river. As the luxuriant landscape grew, so did the Gardners' idea of sharing their home. Architect Cheong Yew Kuan's scheme was to build a series of themed villas, each a composite of independent suites, to evoke the natural elements. Scattered about the 20 acres is "The Source", an award-winning spa, fine restaurants served by produce organically grown on the estate, and yoga and healing specialists who offer a range of treatments. Comfort and service are celebrated keynotes of Begawan Giri but its most precious offering is privacy. "We look forward to guests coming 'home' to stay," says Bradley Gardner.

Begawan Giri Estate ist eine exklusive Enklave, über deren Gästeliste es nur Gerüchte gibt. Donna Karan, Susan Sarandon und Sting waren angeblich hier zu Besuch.

Der englische Unternehmer Bradley Gardner, der seit langem mit Südostasien verbunden ist, entdeckte das überwältigend schöne Gelände. Dort, über einem Tal zwischen zwei Flüssen, wollte er sich ein Ferienhaus bauen. Nach und nach pflanzte er mit seiner Frau Debbie zweitausendfünfhundert Bäume in die hügelige Landschaft und legte unten am Fluss einen Wassergarten an. Während die Flora üppig gedieh, reifte in den Gardners die Idee, die Anlage für Gäste auszubauen. Nach dem Entwurf des Architekten Cheong Yew Kuan wurden einige Villen mit mehreren Suiten gebaut, die sich auf unterschiedliche Weise mit dem Thema Natur auseinandersetzen. Auf dem zehn Hektar großen Gelände liegen außerdem »The Source«, ein preisgekröntes Spa, und erlesene Restaurants, in denen biologische Produkte aus eigenem Anbau serviert werden. Yoga und andere Heilmethoden runden das Angebot ab. Komfort, Service und die Wahrung der Privatsphäre stehen auf Begawan Giri im Mittelpunkt. »Wir wollen, dass unsere Gäste sich bei uns ›zu Hause‹ fühlen«, sagt Bradley Gardner.

Begawan Giri Estate est une enclave si calme et si exclusive que son livre d'or est auréolé de mystère : Donna Karan, Susan Sarandon et Sting y auraient séjourné.

Bradley Gardner, un entrepreneur anglais travaillant depuis longtemps en Asie du Sud-Est, envisageait au départ de construire une résidence secondaire dans ce site qui offre une vue imprenable sur une vallée prise entre deux rivières. Avec Debby, son épouse, il a peu à peu planté 2500 arbres à flanc de coteau et créé un jardin d'eau près de la rivière. A mesure que la végétation luxuriante se développait, l'idée d'accueillir des hôtes a germé dans la tête des Gardner. L'architecte Cheong Yew Kuan a imaginé de construire, sur environ dix hectares, des villas évoquant la nature et comportant chacune des suites indépendantes. Les visiteurs ont à leur disposition un établissement thermal primé appelé « La Source », des restaurants haut de gamme servant des produits bio cultivés sur la propriété, ainsi que des professeurs de yoga et des thérapeutes. Si le confort et la qualité du service ont fait la réputation de Begawan Giri, sa prestation la plus précieuse est la discrétion. « Nous voulons que nos hôtes se sentent chez eux », confie Bradley Gardner.

✲ **PREVIOUS PAGES, CLOCKWISE FROM TOP LEFT** an infinity-edged swimming pool with a floating pavilion in a villa called "Clear Water". Another residence, held aloft by wooden columns, is designed as a tree house. Begawan Giri's terraced water gardens. Wide wooden decks surround a pool in a villa. A massive bath hewn from a single piece of stone. ✲ **VORHERGEHENDE DOPPELSEITEN, IM UHRZEIGERSINN VON OBEN LINKS** ein randloser Swimmingpool mit einem schwebenden Pavillon, genannt»Clear Water«. Eines der Ferienhäuser steht auf hohen Holzsäulen und ist wie ein Baumhaus gebaut. Die stufenförmig angelegten Wassergärten von Begawan Giri. Ausgedehnte Holzterrassen umgeben den Pool einer Villa. Eine riesige Badewanne aus einem einzigen Stein gehauen. ✲ **DOUBLES PAGES PRECEDENTES, DANS LE SENS DES AIGUILLES D'UNE MONTRE, À PARTIR D'EN HAUT À GAUCHE** dans la villa « Eau Claire », une piscine sans bords dotée d'un pavillon flottant. Une maison dans les arbres, construite sur pilotis. Les jardins d'eau étagés de Begawan Giri. De larges terrasses en bois entourent la piscine. Une baignoire massive taillée dans un bloc de pierre.

※ **FACING PAGE** a marble bath bedecked with flower petals in the spa known as "The Source". **ABOVE** The thatched wooden roof in a villa bedroom was inspired by homes in the island of Sumba. A rough-hewn bench from Java stands at the foot of the bed. ※ **LINKE SEITE** eine mit Blüten geschmückte marmorne Badewanne in dem Spa »The Source«. **OBEN** Das hölzerne Strohdach über dem Schlafzimmer einer Villa wurde von Häusern auf der Insel Sumba inspiriert. Eine grob behauene Holzbank aus Java steht am Fußende. ※ **CI-DESSUS, À GAUCHE** Une baignoire en marbre couverte de pétales de fleurs dans le spa « La Source ». **CI-DESSUS** Le toit en bois couvert de chaume de cette chambre est inspiré de l'habitat traditionnel de l'île de Sumba. Au pied du lit, un banc grossièrement taillé.

✳ **ABOVE** Wash basins are set in a massive timber log upheld by rough wooden supports like a village water trough. **RIGHT** a stylish shower in a wood-panelled bathroom. **FACING PAGE** The restaurant called "Kudus House" is housed in an old Javanese wooden building with exquisite carved panels. ✳ **OBEN** Die Waschbecken wurden in einen dicken Baumstamm eingelassen, der auf hölzernen Stützen ruht wie ein bäuerlicher Wassertrog. **RECHTS** eine vornehme Dusche in einem holzgetäfelten Badezimmer. **RECHTE SEITE** Das Restaurant »Kudus House« befindet sich in einem alten javanischen Holzhaus mit feinen holzgeschnitzten Wänden. ✳ **CI-DESSUS** Ces lave-mains creusés dans une pièce de bois massif reposant sur des pieds en bois grossièrement taillés donnent une note rustique. **A DROITE** une douche élégante dans une salle de bains lambrissée. **PAGE DE DROITE** Le restaurant « Kudus House » se trouve dans une construction javanaise ancienne aux superbes panneaux de bois sculptés.

LINDA GARLAND
UBUD BALI

The queen of bamboo in her private forest.

Mention the word bamboo and sooner or later Linda Garland's name will crop up as well. For more than a decade Garland has spearheaded research into every aspect of bamboo, from cultivating new varieties to promoting its use as a sustainable timber and building material of the future.

Linda Garland grew up in Ireland and worked as an interior designer in London before coming to Bali in the early 1970s. She expanded her bamboo-inspired furniture and home furnishings line and quickly became a darling of the jet set with her designs for tropical living: Mick Jagger, Jerry Hall, David Bowie and Richard Branson have all been Garland fans. After taking Indonesian citizenship in 1978, she began to look for a permanent abode, a place of mountain mists and mature trees to remind her of her childhood. Stitching together 35 parcels of land bought from different farmers, she has created a 20-acre estate that straddles a river, a monkey forest and 40 springs that water its sculpted contours. Linda Garland calls her home *Panchoran* which is Balinese for spring waters.

Wenn das Wort Bambus fällt, kommt die Sprache bald auf Linda Garland. Seit über einem Jahrzehnt leitet sie bahnbrechende Forschungen zum Thema Bambus. Dabei geht es ihr um so unterschiedliche Aspekte wie neue Zuchtversuche oder Werbung für das Holz als nachhaltiges und zukunftweisendes Baumaterial.

Linda Garland wuchs in Irland auf und lebte als Innenarchitektin in London, bevor sie in den frühen 1970er Jahren nach Bali kam. Sie baute ihre Linie von Bambus inspirierten Möbeln aus und wurde rasch zum Liebling des Jetset. Garland zählt Mick Jagger, Jerry Hall, David Bowie und Richard Branson zu ihren Kunden. Nachdem sie 1978 indonesische Staatsbürgerin geworden war, suchte sie nach einem Ort inmitten nebelverhangener Berge mit alten Bäumen, der sie an ihre Kindheit erinnerte und wo sie ihren festen Wohnsitz aufschlagen wollte. Sie kaufte mehreren Bauern insgesamt fünfunddreißig Stücke Land ab, die insgesamt zehn Hektar an einem Fluss, einem Affenwald und vierzig Quellen ergaben. Seither lebt sie in ihrem neuen Heim namens *Panchoran*, was auf Balinesisch Frühlingsquellen bedeutet.

Prononcez le mot bambou et le nom de Linda Garland tombe tôt ou tard dans la conversation. Depuis plus d'une décennie, elle est à la pointe de la recherche pour tout ce qui touche au bambou, de la culture de variétés nouvelles à la promotion du bambou en tant que bois d'œuvre et matériau de construction renouvelable du futur.

Linda Garland a grandi en Irlande et travaillé à Londres comme décoratrice, avant de venir à Bali au début des années 1970. Avec sa vaste gamme de meubles et éléments de décoration inspirés du bambou, elle est vite devenue l'enfant chérie de la jet-se: Mick Jagger, Jerry Hall, David Bowie et Richard Branson ont tous été ses fans. Naturalisée indonésienne en 1978, elle s'est mise en quête d'un domicile fixe, perdu dans les brumes des montagnes et les futaies, un endroit qui lui rappelle son enfance. Mettant bout à bout 35 parcelles achetées à des paysans, elle a créé une propriété de dix hectares dans l'enceinte de laquelle on trouve une rivière, une forêt de singes et une quarantaine de sources. C'est pourquoi sa maison s'appelle *Panchoran*, eau de source en balinais.

* **ABOVE** Sunset views from the long main house, which Linda Garland has been extending for 18 years. **BELOW** Her trademark bamboo sofa, inspired by bamboo outriggers on local sailing boats. **FACING PAGE** A thatch-roofed folly built over a river that Linda Garland calls "Jungle Gym". * **OBEN** Blick auf den Sonnenuntergang vom langen Haupthaus aus, das Linda Garland bereits seit achtzehn Jahren erweitert. **UNTEN** Garlands Markensofa aus Bambus, inspiriert von Bambusauslegern auf den Segelbooten der einheimischen Fischer. **RECHTE SEITE** Ein verrücktes Häuschen mit Strohdach wurde über einen Fluss gebaut und von Linda Garland »Jungle Gym« getauft. * **CI-DESSUS** Le coucher de soleil vu de la maison principale que Linda Garland ne cesse d'agrandir depuis 18 ans. **CI-DESSOUS** Le canapé en bambou qui porte sa griffe est inspiré des outriggers équipant les voiliers locaux. **PAGE DE DROITE** Linda Garland a construit une folie au toit de chaume au-dessus d'une rivière, elle l'appelle « Jungle Gym ».

※ **ABOVE** one of the many private reading corners. The black bamboo tray is of traditional design. **FACING PAGE** All the bedrooms open on to open-air showers. ※ **OBEN** eine der vielen geschützten Leseecken. Das schwarze Bambustablett ist in traditionellem Design gehalten. **RECHTE SEITE** Alle Schlafzimmer verfügen über Außenduschen. ※ **CI-DESSUS** un des nombreux endroits où l'on peut se retirer pour lire. Le plateau de bambou noir est de facture traditionnelle. **PAGE DE DROITE** Toutes les chambres donnent sur une douche en plein air.

THE SHRIMP HOUSE
UBUD BALi

A glass-bottomed treasure house.

Access to the Shrimp House is not for the faint-hearted. A spiral staircase of eighty steps descends a cliff face from John and Cynthia Hardy's compound to the rushing Ayung River. Over a path of stepping stones and past a swinging bamboo bridge, one comes upon a serene setting of spring-fed ponds and miniature rice fields.

The Shrimp House is a one-room teak house that John Hardy found in Java and reassembled plank by plank above a pond. As the house was being pieced together he noticed that the teak floor joists framed snapshots of the moving water beneath. Instead of laying a traditional timber floor, he decided to fit panels of tempered glass between the joists. The glass floor provides a fascinating perspective of the pond, now used to breed fresh-water shrimp. For John Hardy, conserving architecture and the environment are part of the same sustainable plan. "Flowing water has been the lifeline of Bali's rice-growing tradition for centuries," he says. "The Shrimp House and its environment honour the landscape while producing food in a natural away."

Der Aufstieg zum »Garnelenhaus« ist anstrengend. Eine Wendeltreppe mit achtzig Stufen führt von einer Felswand auf dem Anwesen von Cynthia und John Hardy hinunter zum Fluss Ayung. Über einen Weg mit Steintritten, vorbei an einer Hängebrücke aus Bambus, gelangt man in eine Idylle aus quellwassergespeisten Teichen und winzigen Reisfeldern.

Das Garnelenhaus besteht aus einem einzigen, in Teakholz gehaltenen Raum, den John Hardy in Java fand und Brett für Brett über dem Teich wieder aufbauen ließ. Dabei bemerkte er, dass man durch die Bodenbretter auf das fließende Wasser sehen konnte. Statt nun einen herkömmlichen Holzboden darüber, ließ er Hartglas-Platten zwischen die Planken legen. Der Glasboden sorgt für einen faszinierenden Ausblick auf den Teich, der inzwischen der Zucht von Süßwassergarnelen dient. Für John Hardy folgt die Bewahrung von Architektur und Umwelt dem Gedanken der Nachhaltigkeit. »Seit Jahrhunderten ist fließendes Wasser die Grundlage der Tradition in Bali, dem Land des Reisanbaus«, sagt er. »Das Garnelenhaus und seine Umgebung respektieren die Landschaft und produzieren gleichzeitig auf natürliche Weise Nahrung.«

Se rendre à la «Maison aux Crevettes», sur les eaux tumultueuses de l'Ayung, demande un certain courage : on y descend par un escalier en colimaçon de 84 marches à flanc de falaise partant de la propriété de John et Cynthia Hardy. Après avoir franchi un gué et un pont suspendu en bambou, on arrive dans un cadre idyllique de bassins d'eau douce et de rizières miniatures.

La «Shrimp House» est une construction en teck, comportant une seule pièce, que John Hardy a trouvée à Java et reconstruite planche par planche au-dessus d'un bassin d'eau douce. Il s'est aperçu au moment du montage que l'on voyait l'eau en mouvement entre les planches. C'est pourquoi il a opté pour des panneaux de verre trempé comme éléments de remplissage, ce qui donne une vue fascinante sur le bassin, dans lequel on élève aujourd'hui des crevettes. Pour John Hardy, conserver l'architecture et préserver l'environnement s'inscrivent dans un programme de développement durable. «L'eau qui coule est depuis des siècles un principe vital de la tradition balinaise fondée sur la riziculture», affirme-t-il. «La Shrimp House et son environnement rendent hommage au site en produisant de la nourriture selon des méthodes naturelles.»

❋ **BELOW** John and Cynthia Hardy with their daughters Carina and Chiara by the fish ponds. **FACING PAGE** View from above onto the Shrimp House. **FOLLOWING PAGES** The Shrimp House is set amid spring-fed rice terraces and fish ponds. ❋ **UNTEN** John und Cynthia Hardy mit ihren Töchtern Carina und Chiara an den Fischteichen. **RECHTE SEITE** Blick von oben auf das Garnelenhaus. **FOLGENDE DOPPELSEITEN** Das Garnelenhaus liegt zwischen Reisterrassen und Fischteichen, die mit Quellwasser versorgt werden. ❋ **CI-DESSOUS** John et Cynthia Hardy avec leurs filles Carina et Chiara, près des bassins à poissons. **PAGE DE DROITE** « La maison aux crevettes », vue d'en haut. **DOUBLE PAGE SUIVANTE** La maison est entourée de bassins à poissons et de rizières irriguées par des sources.

❋ **FACING PAGE** A floor of tempered glass set into old teak floor joists allows an intimate view of the pond beneath. **ABOVE** The century-old walls of the Shrimp House are joined without nails. ❋ **LINKE SEITE** Durch den Hartglas-Boden zwischen den alten Balken aus Teakholz kann man den darunter liegenden Teich aus nächster Nähe betrachten. **OBEN** Die Jahrhunderte alten Wände des Garnelenhauses halten ohne Nägel zusammen. ❋ **PAGE DE GAUCHE** A travers les panneaux de verre trempé montés entre les lattes de teck de l'ancien plancher, on pénètre les secrets du bassin sous la maison. **CI-DESSUS** Les murs centenaires de la « Shrimp House » ont été assemblés sans clous.

JOHN AND CYNTHIA HARDY
UBUD BALI

A visionary creation.

On a piece of land above the Ayung River stands the Hardy house – one of the most famous in Bali, a collaboration between Malaysian architect Cheong Yew Kuan and John Hardy, the jewellery designer.

Based on the concept of a Borneo longhouse, the structure soars above the garden on ironwood posts, many of them old electricity poles brought, in fact, from Borneo. "It's all about the wood," says Hardy, a Canadian who came to Bali in 1975 and together with his wife Cynthia established a well-known brand name in jewellery. "I brought together the materials and Yew Kuan assembled them with the hands of an angel." Raw tree trunks, rafters of peeled clove logs and tea tree trunks were raised on tiers of bamboo scaffolding. The Hardys wanted to use natural materials that respected the landscape. The house has no walls; the lower storey is almost completely open and glass windows along the upper floor fold back to tropical breezes and panoramic views of rice fields and the river. Brilliantly simple, it is a house that harbours no secrets.

Auf einem Hügel über dem Fluss Ayung steht das auf Bali berühmte Haus der Hardys – ein Gemeinschaftswerk von John Hardy, dem Schmuckdesigner, und Cheong Yew Kuan, einem Architekten aus Malaysia.

Wie bei den Langhäusern auf Borneo steht das Gebäude auf Eisenholzpfeilern über dem Garten. Einige sind übrigens ehemalige Strommasten aus Borneo. »Das hat alles mit dem Holz zu tun«, sagt der Kanadier Hardy, der 1975 nach Bali kam und mit seiner Frau Cynthia eine Schmuckproduktion mit einem mittlerweile bekannten Markennamen aufbaute. »Ich habe das Material besorgt und Yew Kuan hat es mit Engelshänden zusammengestellt.« Rohe Baumstämme, Gebälk aus geschälten gespaltenen Baumstämmen und Teebaumstämme – alles wurde über stufenförmig angelegte Bambusgerüste hoch geschafft. Die Hardys bevorzugten aus Respekt vor der Landschaft natürliches Baumaterial. Das Haus hat keine Mauern; die untere Etage bleibt fast vollständig offen, während die Glasscheiben im zweiten Stockwerk zurückgeschlagen werden können, wenn man die tropische Brise oder den Panoramablick auf die Reisfelder und den Fluss genießen will.

Sur une parcelle dominant l'Ayung se trouve la maison des Hardy, fruit de la collaboration entre l'architecte malais Cheong Yew Kuan et John Hardy, créateur de bijoux.

Construit sur le modèle des maisons longues de Bornéo, le bâtiment s'élève au-dessus du jardin sur des poteaux de bois de fer, dont la plupart sont d'ailleurs d'anciens poteaux électriques de Bornéo. « Tout tourne autour du bois », explique Hardy, Canadien installé à Bali depuis 1975 et qui s'est fait avec son épouse Cynthia un nom dans le monde de la bijouterie. «J'ai réuni les matériaux et Yew Kuan les a assemblés avec des doigts de fée», dit-il. Des troncs d'arbres bruts, des chevrons faits de souches de giroflier pelées et de troncs de melaleuca ont été montés sur des échafaudages de bambou. Les Hardy voulaient des matériaux naturels qui respectent l'environnement. La maison est dépourvue de murs : le niveau inférieur est presque entièrement ouvert tandis que les baies vitrées de l'étage supérieur s'esquivent devant les brises tropicales et les vues panoramiques sur les rizières et la rivière. Cette maison d'une simplicité admirable ne dissimule aucun secret.

❋ **PREVIOUS PAGES** views of the house from entrance gate to the rice fields beyond. The house at dusk, lit by hundreds of beeswax candles. **FACING PAGE** The central staircase acts as a giant brace to stabilize the house. It is covered in mud using an old Balinese technique. **RIGHT** Roots of jungle plants lean against a sleeping room roofed with mosquito netting. **BELOW** The tree trunks used as braces were found in Java. **FOLLOWING PAGES** The woven bamboo wall in the dining area is in the style of houses on the island of Madura. Cushions are covered in fabric used for monks' robes in Thailand. ❋ **VORHERGE-HENDE DOPPELSEITEN** Blick vom Eingangstor auf das Haus und die dahinter liegenden Reisfelder. In der Abenddämmerung wird das Haus mit hunderten von Bienenwachskerzen beleuchtet. **LINKE SEITE** Die Haupttreppe dient gleichzeitig als gewaltige Stütze für die Stabilität des Hauses. Das Holz wurde nach einer alten balinesischen Technik mit Schlamm überzogen. **RECHTS** Die Wurzeln von Dschungelpflanzen lehnen an einem Schlafzimmer, dessen Decke aus einem Moskitonetz besteht. **UNTEN** Die stützenden Baumstämme stammen aus Java. **FOLGENDE DOPPELSEITEN** Geflochtene Bambuswände wie hier im Esszimmer findet man auf der Insel Madura. Die Kissenstoffe werden ursprünglich für Mönchsroben in Thailand benutzt. ❋ **DOUBLES PAGES PRECEDENTES** la maison vue du portail d'entrée, avec les rizières en arrière-plan. Le soir, des centaines de bougies en cire d'abeille illuminent la maison. **PAGE DE GAUCHE** L'escalier central tient lieu d'étai géant qui stabilise la maison. La colonne a été recouverte de boue selon une technique balinaise ancienne. **A DROITE** Les racines de plantes tropicales prennent appui sur le mur d'une chambre dotée d'un toit-moustiquaire. **CI-DESSOUS** Les troncs d'arbre servant de support proviennent de Java. **DOUBLES PAGES SUIVANTES** La cloison en bambou tressé de la salle à manger est typique de l'habitat de Madura. Le tissu des coussins sert à confectionner les robes des moines thaïlandais.

❋ **ABOVE** Stepping stones across the fish pond connect the living room to a guest cottage. **BELOW** Upstairs, the hall is floored with poles of hard swamp wood. **FACING PAGE** an open pavilion in the garden. ❋ **OBEN** Die Steinstufen verbinden den Fischteich mit dem Wohnzimmer und einem Gästehäuschen. **UNTEN** Der Fußboden der oberen Etage besteht aus Stämmen des harten Treibholzes. **RECHTE SEITE** ein offener Gartenpavillon. ❋ **CI-DESSUS** Un gué relie le salon et un pavillon pour les invités. **CI-DESSOUS** A l'étage, le sol est fait de bois des marais pétrifié. **PAGE DE DROITE** Le pavillon du jardin est ouvert aux quatre vents.

❈ **ABOVE** A Chinese wedding bed in the dining area is used for seating. **FACING PAGE** The dining room's woven bamboo wall is hung with children's ceremonial jackets from Sumatra. ❈ **OBEN** Im Essbereich kann man sich auf diesem chinesischen Hochzeitsbett niederlassen. **RECHTE SEITE** An der geflochtenen Wand im Esszimmer hängen Zeremonienjacken von Kindern aus Sumatra. ❈ **CI-DESSUS** Dans l'espace repas, on s'assied sur un lit nuptial chinois. **PAGE DE DROITE** Des vestes de cérémonie d'enfants de Sumatra sont pendues au mur de bambou tissé de la salle à manger.

※ **ABOVE** The hand-beaten copper kitchen sink is set in a mahogany table. **RIGHT** The draperies in the bedroom are made from fine muslin used to strain tofu. **FACING PAGE** The bath tub overlooks a vista of rice fields. **FOLLOWING PAGES** The bed was crafted from salvaged lengths of teak and ironwood. A collection of old copper pots at the main entrance. ※ **OBEN** Das handgehämmerte Kupferbecken ist in den Mahagonitisch eingelassen. **RECHTS** Die Vorhänge im Schlafzimmer sind aus feinem Musselin, das normalerweise zum Seihen von Tofu verwendet wird. **RECHTE SEITE** Von der Badewanne aus kann man über die Reisfelder schauen. **FOLGENDE DOPPELSEITEN** Das Bett wurde aus geborgenen Teak- und Eisenholzstämmen gebaut. Alte Kupfertöpfe am Haupteingang. ※ **CI-DESSUS** L'évier en cuivre martelé à la main est encastré dans une table en acajou. **A DROITE** Les voilages de la chambre sont en mousseline; la même sert à égoutter le tofu. **PAGE DE DROITE** On peut contempler les rizières en prenant son bain. **DOUBLES PAGES SUIVANTES** Le lit est en teck et bois de fer de récupération. Une collection d'urnes en cuivre anciennes à l'entrée.

AN OLD JAVA HOUSE
UBUD BALI

A prize jewel in teak.

This tiny jewel of a house is about a hundred years old and was once the home of a minor Javanese court official.

John and Cynthia Hardy found the one-room residence being used as a storeroom in a row of concrete houses. It was rescued, dismantled, transported to Bali and re-assembled by carpenters on its own little plot of land in the Hardy compound. Though modest, its intricately carved interior attests to its importance. It must have seemed imposing a century ago in comparison with the woven bamboo huts that surrounded it. Traces of the original blue paint still tint the exterior walls. The walls and beams are hand-hewn slabs of solid teak, resistant to insect damage. Few nails are used and the floor boards are joined with wooden pegs. A deck of old teak planks embraces the single room, though a small bathroom has been subtly incorporated in one corner. Lovingly restored, and shaded by young teak trees, the Old Java House now enjoys a dignified retirement under the stewardship of the Hardys.

Dieses kleine Juwel ist ungefähr hundert Jahre alt und gehörte einst einem javanischen Hofbeamten niederen Ranges.

Als John und Cynthia Hardy das Häuschen, das aus einem einzigen Raum besteht, zwischen Betongebäuden entdeckten, diente es als Lager. Sie ließen es vollständig demontieren und nach Bali bringen, wo es von Schreinern auf dem Anwesen der Hardys wieder aufgebaut wurde. Trotz seiner bescheidenen Erscheinung kann man von den komplizierten Schnitzereien im Inneren auf eine gewisse Bedeutung schließen. Vor einem Jahrhundert muss es zwischen den damals üblichen Bambushütten aufgefallen sein. An den Außenwänden sind noch Spuren der einst blauen Färbung sichtbar. Die Wände und Balken bestehen aus mit der Hand bearbeitetem harten Teakholz, dem Insekten nichts anhaben können. Es wurden kaum Nägel eingeschlagen, und die Bodendielen werden nur durch Zapfen zusammen gehalten. Eine Terrasse aus alten Teakbrettern schmiegt sich an das Häuschen, und in einer Ecke wurde ein kleines Badezimmer eingebaut. Das liebevoll restaurierte alte javanische Haus hat so im Schatten junger Teakbäume einen würdigen Platz gefunden.

Cette ravissante maisonnette qui a près d'un siècle était naguère habitée par un petit magistrat javanais.

Lorsque John et Cynthia Hardy l'ont découverte, cette demeure d'une seule pièce, coincée dans une rangée de maisons en béton, servait d'entrepôt. Ils l'ont fait démonter, transporter à Bali et rassembler par des charpentiers à l'emplacement qu'elle occupe actuellement. Malgré ses dimensions réduites, son intérieur finement sculpté atteste son importance. Il y a un siècle, elle devait avoir fière allure comparée aux huttes de bambou tressé qui l'entouraient. Des traces de la peinture bleue d'origine sont encore visibles sur les murs extérieurs. Les murs et poutres ont été taillés à la main dans des blocs de teck robuste, résistant aux attaques des insectes. On a limité l'utilisation de clous et assemblé les lattes du plancher au moyen de chevilles en bois. Un pont de vieilles planches de teck court tout autour de la maison, seulement interrompu par une salle de bains judicieusement aménagée dans un angle. Restaurée avec amour, cette ancienne maison de Java à l'ombre de jeunes tecks vit maintenant une paisible retraite chez les Hardy.

✳ **ABOVE** Traces of the original paint are visible on the airy front porch of the Old Java House. **RIGHT** Sequestered from the garden by wooden screens, the bathroom uses a primitive Javanese ladder as a towel rack. **FACING PAGE** The carved wall decorations are perfectly preserved . ✳ **OBEN** Auf der luftigen Veranda des javanischen Häuschens erkennt man noch Spuren der Originalfarbe. **RECHTS** Die Holz-wände schirmen das Bad gegen den Garten ab. Eine schlichte javanische Leiter dient als Handtuchhal-ter. **RECHTE SEITE** Die holzgeschnitzten Wandverzierungen sind vollständig erhalten. ✳ **CI-DESSUS** La pein-ture bleue d'origine est encore visible dans l'entrée ouverte. **A DROITE** Dans la salle de bains isolée du jardin par un paravent en bois, une échelle sommaire sert de porte-serviettes. **CI-DESSUS** dans la salle de bains de plein air, une table de toilette en bois de palme noir et un vieux cheval á ba saule Javanais.

AULIA'S HOUSE

CANGGU BALI

A revival of rural style.

Set in a family compound contained in a wider landscape of rice paddies, waving coconut palms and banana trees, Aulia's house sprouts out of the fertile soil, a compact and organic growth.

In a way it has indeed sprouted: it is a piece-by-piece reconstruction of an old rural dwelling in Bali; the timber frame, panels and stilts put back like a jigsaw under a pitched roof of terra cotta tiles. For Aulia, a Sumatran who has lived in Bali for many years, it is also the logical extension of a life-long quest of collecting many of the remaining or abandoned deposits of an ancient rural culture – stone pillars and troughs, wooden beams and panels, articles of everyday use and objects of ritual art, such as the two polychrome wooden heads of sacred bulls, seen left, that are venerated in Bali's Hindu myths. Elsewhere, Aulia's reconstructed barns and dwellings would be put in a museum. But with perseverance and foresight he has managed to save them in the very habitat from which they sprang.

Aulias Haus scheint auf dem Familienanwesen, das in eine weite Landschaft mit Reisfeldern, sich wiegenden Kokospalmen und Bananenstauden eingebettet ist, aus dem fruchtbaren Boden herauszuwachsen.

Und in gewissem Sinn stimmt das, denn das Haus wurde Stück für Stück aus einem alten ländlichen balinesischen Gebäude wie ein Puzzle aus Fachwerk, Brettern und Pfählen wieder zusammengesetzt. Auf die Neukonstruktion wurde ein Dach aus Terrakottaziegeln gesetzt. Für Aulia, der aus Sumatra stammt, aber schon lange in Bali lebt, ist das Haus die logische Fortsetzung einer lebenslangen Sammelleidenschaft für ausrangierte oder vernachlässigte Überreste der alten ländlichen Kultur. Viele dieser Gegenstände finden sich nun im oder am Haus wieder: Steinsäulen, Tröge, Holzbalken und -bretter, alltägliche und rituelle Utensilien, wie die beiden bunten Holzköpfe heiliger Stiere (linke Seite), die in den Hindumythen Balis verehrt werden. In anderen Ländern würden Aulias restaurierte Scheunen und Gebäude in einem Museum ausgestellt werden. Hier aber ist es ihm durch Hartnäckigkeit und Weitblick gelungen, sie in ihrer ursprünglichen Umgebung zu erhalten.

Dans une propriété familiale parmi les rizières, les cocotiers et les bananiers ondoyants, la maison d'Aulia surgit de la terre fertile, telle une pousse drue et naturelle.

Et c'est vrai en un sens puisqu'il s'agit de la reconstitution pièce par pièce d'une vieille demeure rurale balinaise ; sa charpente, ses panneaux et ses pilotis en bois ont été remontés à la manière d'un puzzle sous un toit en pente recouvert de tuiles en terre cuite. Pour Aulia, originaire de Sumatra et installé à Bali depuis de nombreuses années, c'est dans la logique de toute une vie passée à collectionner des trésors délaissés ou négligés d'une civilisation rurale ancienne : piliers et auges en pierre, poutres et panneaux en bois, objets courants ou rituels, comme les deux têtes de taureaux sacrés en bois polychromes (voir illustration à gauche), qui sont vénérés dans les mythes hindouistes balinais. Partout ailleurs, les granges et maisons reconstituées d'Aulia seraient conservées dans des musées. Mais visionnaire persévérant, Aulia est parvenu à les préserver dans leur environnement d'origine.

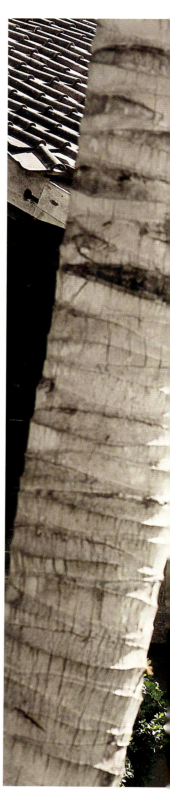

* **FACING PAGE** The simple rural dwelling is furnished with village furniture. A rice barn with its thatched roof of *alang alang* grass. **ABOVE** the shaded sit-out of the reconstructed peasant home. **FOLLOWING PAGES** on the veranda, a traditional wooden water trough. * **LINKE SEITE** ein sonnengeschütztes Plätzchen vor dem restaurierten Bauernhaus. Eine Reisscheune – das Strohdach ist mit *alang-alang*-Gras gedeckt. **OBEN** Das schlichte Bauernhaus ist mit Möbeln aus dem Ort eingerichtet. **FOLGENDE DOPPELSEITE** Auf der Veranda steht ein traditioneller hölzerner Waschtrog. * **PAGE DE GAUCHE** La maison paysanne est meublée très simplement. Le grenier à riz est surmonté d'un toit en *alang alang*. **CI-DESSUS** La terrasse ombragée de la maison paysanne reconstituée. **DOUBLE PAGE SUIVANTE** Un abreuvoir traditionnel agrémente la véranda.

Carolina Tety
Canggu Bali

Art and nature in harmonious unison.

Carolina Tety comes from Jakarta but moved to Bali as a young woman. Here she married and started a family. Her former husband Aulia and she opened a store selling furniture and traditional art.

As the young couple scoured the villages of the countryside and outlying islands for goods to stock, a simple idea struck them on a trip to the Javan heartland. A tall, imposing *lumbung*, a rice barn, was available for purchase. Why not reassemble it into a home? One thing led to another and before long the couple had acquired several whole and partial dwellings. Architects were inadequate to the task of reassembling wooden beams, columns and walls of teak panels, often without the use of nails. Carolina and Aulia sought out village builders and artisans. Fitting the old floorboards smoothly, she recalls, was hardest of all. They put their home in a compound, filling it with primitive art, rustic objects and furniture of their own devising. The house is in one of the quieter parts of Bali and at night you can hear the sea and be transported by its murmur.

Carolina Tety stammt aus Jakarta, zog aber bereits als junge Frau nach Bali. Zusammen mit ihrem Ex-Mann Aulia handelte sie mit Möbeln und traditionellen Kunstwerken.

Während das junge Paar die Dörfer auf dem Land und vorgelagerte Inseln nach passender Ware durchforsteten, kam ihnen auf einer Reise ins javanische Herzland eine einfache Idee. Eine hohe mächtige *lumbung*, eine Reisscheune, stand zum Verkauf. Sie beschlossen, sie in ein Wohngebäude umzubauen. Eins führte zum Anderen, und kurz darauf hatte das Ehepaar mehrere vollständig oder teilweise erhaltene ländliche Gebäude erworben. Architekten stellten sich als ungeeignet heraus, hölzerne Balken und Säulen sowie die Teakbretter, möglichst ohne Nägel, neu zusammenzusetzen. Und so engagierten Carolina und Aulia Bauarbeiter und Handwerker aus dem Ort. In ihrer Erinnerung war es das Schwierigste, die alten Bodenbretter passend einzufügen. Sie stellten ihr Haus auf ein größeres Anwesen in der quirligsten Gegend Balis und richteten es mit naiver Kunst, ländlichen Objekten und selbst entworfenen Möbeln ein. Nachts kann man das Meer rauschen hören und sich durch sein Murmeln in die Träume tragen lassen.

Originaire de Jakarta, Carolina Tety s'est installée à Bali dans sa jeunesse. Avec son ex-mari Aulia, elle a monté un magasin d'art traditionnel et de meubles achetés à la campagne et dans les îles au large de Bali.

C'est à l'occasion d'une expédition au cœur de Java qu'une idée toute simple leur a traversé l'esprit : un lumbung imposant, un grenier à riz, était à vendre. Pourquoi ne pas en faire une maison? De fil en aiguille, le jeune couple a rapidement fait l'acquisition de maisons entières et de matériaux de récupération. Plutôt qu'à des architectes, c'est à des bâtisseurs et artisans du village que Carolina et Aulia ont confié la tâche de remonter des poutres en bois, des colonnes et des panneaux de teck, souvent sans utiliser de clous. «Assembler les panneaux en bois des sols a été le plus dur», se souvient-elle. Ils ont installé leur maison sur un terrain clos et l'ont remplie d'art primitif, d'objets rustiques et de mobilier de leur propre création. La maison est située dans un des endroits les plus calmes de Bali, et la nuit, on peut entendre la mer et se laisser transporter par sa musique.

❋ **PREVIOUS PAGES** a rice barn in the tree-filled compound. **FACING PAGE** A freestanding gateway of stone and wood leads into the open-plan living room. Wooden staves, beams and functional stone pieces are scattered in the open-air bathing area. **ABOVE** The steps to the raised pool echo a *lumbung's* steps. ❋ **VORHERGEHENDE DOPPELSEITE** eine Reisscheune auf dem mit Bäumen bepflanzten Anwesen. **LINKE SEITE** Ein freistehender Torbogen aus Stein und Holz führt in das offen angelegte Wohnzimmer. Balken und andere ehemals nützliche Teile aus Holz und Stein sind auf dem Badegelände unter freiem Himmel verstreut. Gedenkfiguren bewachen das Anwesen. **OBEN** Die Treppe zu dem erhöhten Swimmingpool erinnert an *lumbung*-Leitern. ❋ **DOUBLE PAGE PRECEDENTE** un grenier à riz sur la propriété très arborée. **PAGE DE GAUCHE** Une entrée en bois et pierre mène au salon ouvert. Des poutres en bois ainsi que des objets utilitaires sout disséminés dans la propriété at l'espace en plein air. **CI-DESSUS** L'échelle qui mène à la piscine surélevée évoque les escaliers du *lumbung*.

❋ **PREVIOUS PAGES** view of the central pavilion of the house that is the main living and dining area. **FACING PAGE** The village bed is made from massive, rough-hewn timbers. An arrangement of primitive art in wood and stone below the staircase. **ABOVE** a massive piece of teak placed on wooden blocks forms a simple table. ❋ **VORHERGEHENDE DOPPELSEITE** Blick auf den Hauptpavillon des Hauses mit dem Wohn- und Essbereich. **LINKE SEITE** Das traditionelle Bett ist aus massivem, roh behauenem Holz. Unter der Treppe eine Ansammlung naiver Kunstwerke aus Holz und Stein. **OBEN** Der schlichte Tisch besteht aus einer massiven Teakholzplatte, die auf mächtigen Holzbalken aufliegt. ❋ **DOUBLE PAGE PRECEDENTE** Le pavillon central de la maison abritant le salon et la salle à manger. **PAGE DE GAUCHE** un lit paysan en bois massif grossièrement taillé. Des objets de l'art primitif en bois et pierre sont disposés près de l'escalier. **CI-DESSUS** Un bloc de teck posé sur des billots de bois fait une table toute simple.

BaLi

Colonial cool meets contemporary chic.

The owner of this house, who travels widely, wanted a contemporary look in a house that incorporated some key features of Balinese architecture: a colonial-style veranda, a tree-lined courtyard with a swimming pool and, above all, a practical, functional home with lots of light and air that would be easy to maintain.

Built on a 1000 sq. metre plot in Seminyak, the house occupies less than half that area, the rest being left open for casual outdoor living. Simplicity is the keynote. Clean straight lines and a monochromatic colour scheme emphasise the lack of clutter. Carefully chosen antiques co-habit with modern pieces – including artworks by visiting artist friends – with cosmopolitan flair. The front door, left, has handles found in Morocco and opens to reveal an old carved Indonesian panel at the end of the corridor. The whole effect is of living lightly – as in an air bubble. This house in Seminyak has all the charm, comfort and good taste associated with Modern Bali.

Die weit gereiste Besitzerin wünschte sich ein Haus mit zeitgenössischem Ausdruck, das einige Kernelemente balinesischer Architektur aufweisen sollte: eine Veranda im Kolonialstil, einen Innenhof mit Swimmingpool und Bäumen; vor allem aber ein praktisches und pflegeleichtes Haus mit viel Licht und Luft.

Das Haus nimmt auf einem 1000 Quadratmeter großen Grundstück in Seminyak weniger als die Hälfte des verfügbaren Platzes ein. Die verbleibende Fläche lädt dazu ein, sich unter freiem Himmel zu vergnügen. Einfachheit heißt das Leitmotiv, und die klaren Linien sowie die Konzentration auf eine einzige Farbe betonen den Verzicht auf alles Überflüssige. Sorgsam ausgewählte Antiquitäten wurden mit modernen Objekten mit kosmopolitischem Flair kombiniert – darunter Arbeiten von Künstlern, die zu Besuch kamen. Die Klinken an der Eingangstür stammen aus Marokko, und am Ende des Flurs erkennt man eine alte geschnitzte indonesische Holzvertäfelung (linke Seite). Hier lebt es sich leicht – wie in einer Luftblase. Das Haus in Seminyak verfügt über all den Charme, Komfort und guten Geschmack, den man mit dem modernen Bali verbindet.

La propriétaire de cette maison, grande voyageuse, voulait créer une maison au look contemporain qui intègre certains éléments clés de l'architecture balinaise : une véranda de style colonial, une cour bordée d'arbres avec piscine. Ce devait avant tout être une maison pratique et fonctionnelle, qui soit aérée, lumineuse et facile à entretenir.

Construite sur un terrain de 1 000 m^2 à Seminyak, elle occupe moins de la moitié de cette surface, le reste invitant à savourer la vie en plein air. La simplicité est la note générale. Des lignes claires et pures et l'ambiance monochrome accentuent le dépouillement. Des antiquités choisies avec soin cohabitent avec des œuvres modernes de style cosmopolite – certaines ont été réalisées par des amis artistes lors de visites. La porte d'entrée en placage est dotée de poignées trouvées au Maroc et ouvre sur un couloir au fond duquel se trouve sculpté indonésien ancien (page de gauche). Le tout donne une impression de légèreté, comme si on était dans une bulle d'air. Cette maison a tout le charme, le confort et la classe qu'on associe au Bali moderne.

✳ **ABOVE** The corridor is a progression of space between the entrance and the main house. **FACING PAGE** An old Balinese door with its patina of crumbling paint opens into the colonnaded veranda. ✳ **OBEN** Der ausgedehnte Flur führt vom Eingang zum Haupthaus. **RECHTE SEITE** Eine alte balinesische Tür mit der Patina uralter Farbe geht auf die säulengeschmückte Terrasse hinaus. ✳ **CI-DESSUS** Le long couloir mène de l'entrée à la maison principale. **PAGE DE DROITE** Une porte balinaise ancienne à la peinture patinée par les ans donne sur la véranda à péristyle.

✻ **FACING PAGE** a tea table set by the side of the pool. a guest room with an antique four-poster brass bed. **ABOVE** The living room, with vases filled with tuberoses, is enlivened with art-works by Singapore artist Lu Guo Xiang who painted them while staying here as a guest. **FOLLOWING PAGES** Hardwood village furniture by the aquamarine pool adds a rustic touch. ✻ **LINKE SEITE** Tee am Swimmingpool – der Gipfel der Entspannung! Ein Gästezimmer mit einem antiken Himmelbett aus Messing. **OBEN** Im Wohnzimmer stehen Vasen mit Tuberosen. Die Bilder malte der Singapurer Künstler Lu Guo Xiang, während er zu Besuch war. **FOLGENDE DOPPELSEITE** Schlichte Hartholzmöbel am Swimmingpool verleihen der Anlage einen rustikalen Anstrich. ✻ **PAGE DE GAUCHE** une table basse pour le thé au bord de la piscine. La chambre d'amis est dotée d'un lit à baldaquin ancien en laiton. **CI-DESSUS** Des œuvres réalisées par l'artiste singapourien Lu Guo Xiang à l'occasion d'une visite mettent de la couleur dans le salon, où l'on remarque des vases remplis de tubéreuses. **DOUBLE PAGE SUIVANTE** Des meubles en bois dur, près de la piscine, donnent une note rustique à l'ensemble.

❋ **ABOVE** a Balinese pavilion with its roof of *alang alang* grass by the poolside. **RIGHT** an old wooden panel above a bamboo bench on the veranda. **FACING PAGE** Frangipani trees shade an old wooden relaxing chair. Beyond is the thatched-roof pavilion. ❋ **OBEN** Ein balinesischer Pavillon, der mit *alang-alang*-Gras gedeckt ist, bietet Schatten am Pool. **RECHTS** Eine alte Holzvertäfelung hängt über einer Bambusbank auf der Terrasse. **RECHTE SEITE** Pagodenbäume geben dem alten Liegestuhl aus Holz Schatten. Dahinter steht der Pavillon mit dem Strohdach. ❋ **CI-DESSUS** Un pavillon balinais surmonté d'un toit en *alang alang* au bord de la piscine. **A DROITE** Un panneau de bois ancien au-dessus d'un banc de bambou sur la véranda. **PAGE DE DROITE** Une chaise de repos ancienne à l'ombre des frangipaniers. A l'arrière-plan, le pavillon au toit de chaume.

ANNEKE'S GUESTHOUSE
UBUD BALI

A jasmine-scented oasis.

"In the West, where I come from, we live in closed houses to protect ourselves from rain, wind and snow. Here, my mind floats with the rising sun. I live and sleep with nature, the sun and the moon ...," says Anneke van Waesberghe of her guesthouse in Payogan, Ubud.

Situated between a river and a tree-filled gorge, it is a resting place for the contemporary nomad. The simple two-storeyed structure has a straw roof of *alang alang* grass and an open living interior on the ground floor, a room without walls. The furniture is multi-functional: a platform and cushions that face east and west. Waking to the sound of birdsong and the scent of frangipani, one takes in the sunrise and dawdles over breakfast. In the evening the cushions are reversed for sunset views. Upstairs, in a room of generouse size, the study area (left) is screened from the Chinese-style bamboo bed by a light curtain (following pages). The white-painted floor boards go with the snowy bed linen and drapes of gauzy mosquito netting. It is all a restless romantic needs.

»Wo ich herkomme, leben wir in geschlossenen Häusern, um uns vor Regen, Wind und Schnee zu schützen. Hier schwingt meine Seele im Einklang mit der aufgehenden Sonne. Ich lebe und schlafe im Rhythmus der Natur, der Sonne und des Mondes ...«, sagt Anneke van Waesberghe, die Betreiberin der Pension in Payogan, Ubud.

Das erholsame Gästehaus für moderne Nomaden liegt zwischen einem Fluss und einer bewaldeten Schlucht. Das zweistöckige Hauses ist mit einem Strohdach aus *alang-alang*-Gras gedeckt. Der offene Wohnbereich im Erdgeschoss hat keine Wände; die multifunktionale Einrichtung besteht aus einem erhöhten Podest mit vielen Kissen, das nach Osten und Westen ausgerichtet ist. Schon beim Aufwachen kann man zum Duft von Frangipani Vögel singen hören und anschließend beim Frühstück in aller Seelenruhe den Sonnenaufgang bewundern. Abends werden die Kissen in Richtung Sonnenuntergang umgedreht. In dem großen Zimmer im ersten Stock (linke Seite) kann man zwischen dem Arbeitsraum und dem Bambusbett in chinesischem Stil einen Vorhang ziehen (folgende Doppelseite). Der weiß getünchte Dielenboden passt gut zu dem schneeweißen Bett und den hauchfeinen Moskitonetzen. Was will ein rastloser Romantiker mehr?

«En Occident, là où je suis née, nous vivons dans des maisons fermées pour nous protéger de la pluie, du vent et de la neige. Ici mon âme s'élève avec le soleil. Je vis et dors avec la nature, le soleil et la lune ...», dit Annecke van Waesberghe de sa pension à Payogan, près d'Ubud.

Située entre une rivière et une gorge densément boisée, c'est un lieu de repos pour les nomades des temps modernes. Cette construction simple à deux niveaux est coiffée d'un toit en *alang alang* et dotée au rez-de-chaussée d'une pièce de séjour ouverte, sans murs. L'estrade et les coussins orientés est-ouest sont multifonctionnels : le matin, on se réveille avec le chant des oiseaux et le parfum des frangipaniers et on savoure son petit-déjeuner ; le soir, on change les coussins de direction pour jouir du coucher de soleil. A l'étage, dans une pièce aux proportions généreuses, un fin rideau sépare le coin bureau (page de gauche) du lit en bambou de style chinois (double page suivante). Le plancher peint en blanc s'accorde avec la note immaculée des draps et de la mousseline retombant en drapé de la moustiquaire. C'est tout ce dont a besoin une romantique ne tenant pas en place.

Anneke van Waesberghe
UBUD BALi

A traveller's essentials.

For 20 years of her life, Anneke van Waesberghe raced round the world, airline tickets bulging in her pocket. When people asked her where she lived, she was dumbfounded for a precise answer.

She ran an organization that brought together architects and designers from Japan and the western world. There came a point when it all seemed slightly unreal. Reality dawned when she found a new life and vocation in Bali. From her accumulated list of travellers' tales, and the newfound experience of creating a permanent home, was born "Esprit Nomade", a label that designs and markets a wide range of travellers' accessories. From the company's elegant logo enshrined at the entrance to her home, left, to portable mosquito nets, canvas furniture, tented cabinets and a variety of loungewear shown in the following pages, Anneke's trademark style fills her home. She has never been happier: putting down her roots in a rich soil, creating with Bali's skilled artisans and sharing her breezy house with Mickey the cat, who always finds the most comfortable spot.

20 Jahre lang sauste Anneke van Waesberghe rund um die Welt, bis die Flugtickets ihre Taschen ausbeulten. Wenn man sie fragte, wo sie wohnte, war sie daher oft um eine Antwort verlegen.

Sie leitete ein Unternehmen, das japanische Architekten und Designer mit Kollegen aus dem Westen zusammenbrachte. Eines Tages erschien ihr das alles unwirklich. Die Wirklichkeit fand sie jedoch wieder, als sie in Bali einen neuen Anfang machte – privat und geschäftlich. Aus den vielen erlebten Reisegeschichten und der neuen Erfahrung, sich endgültig niederzulassen, entstand »Esprit Nomade«, ein Label, unter dem vielfältigste Reiseaccessoires vertrieben werden. Vom eleganten Firmenlogo am Eingang ihres Hauses (linke Seite) über Reise-Moskitonetze, Segeltuchmöbel und Zeltschränke bis hin zu einem breiten Angebot an Straßenkleidung – Annekes Stil ist im Haus allgegenwärtig. Und sie selbst ist glücklicher denn je, seit sie in dem fruchtbaren Boden Wurzeln geschlagen hat, mit geschickten balinesischen Handwerkern ihre Kreationen entwickelt und ihr luftiges Haus mit Kater Mickey teilt, der immer ein bequemes Plätzchen findet.

20 ans de sa vie, Anneke van Waesberghe a parcouru le monde, les poches bourrées de billets d'avion. Quand on lui demandait où elle habitait, elle était bien en peine de répondre.

Elle dirigeait une organisation favorisant les rencontres entre des architectes et des designers japonais et occidentaux. Et puis, un beau jour, tout cela lui a semblé assez illusoire. Mais la réalité s'est imposée à elle quand elle a découvert une nouvelle vie à Bali et y a trouvé une vocation. «Esprit Nomade», marque d'accessoires pour le voyage, est né de ses nombreuses aventures et de l'expérience de sa sédentarisation. Du logo de l'entreprise inscrit dans la pierre à l'entrée de sa maison (page de gauche), aux moustiquaires portables, en passant par des meubles de rangement ressemblant à des tentes et par des vêtements d'intérieur, le style Esprit Nomade est omniprésent chez Anneke. Jamais elle n'a été aussi heureuse : elle s'enracine dans une terre fertile, travaille avec des artisans balinais qualifiés et partage sa maison ventilée avec le chat Mickey, qui trouve toujours l'endroit le plus confortable.

※ **ABOVE** A bedroom on the upper floor is draped with a mosquito net of voile. The hat is from Vietnam and the lacquer thermos flask from Myanmar. **RIGHT AND FACING PAGE** The open-air shower is an extension of the bathroom, both made of white concrete. ※ **OBEN** Das Schlafzimmer im ersten Stock ist mit Moskitonetzen aus Voile ausgestattet. Der Hut stammt aus Vietnam, die Lack-Thermosflasche aus Myanmar. **RECHTS UND RECHTE SEITE** Die Außendusche schließt sich ans Badezimmer an. Beide Räume wurden aus weißem Beton erbaut. ※ **CI-DESSUS** Le lit à l'étage supérieur est enveloppé dans une moustiquaire en voile. Le chapeau vient du Vietnam et la bouteille thermos de Myanmar. **A DROITE ET PAGE DE DROITE** La douche en plein air se trouve dans le prolongement de la salle de bains. Toutes deux sont en béton blanc.

Taman Bebek
Sayan Bali

An enchanted Balinese Garden.

Since the mid-1970s, Australian-born Made Wijaya – a.k.a. Michael White – has been as much part of the Bali scene as a rice paddy or a village shrine. Architect, garden designer, tennis coach and, above all, an inveterate chronicler of goings-on in cosmopolitan Bali, he is both the island's sought-after gadfly and adopted godson.

In innumerable articles and books Wijaya has portrayed a wide spectrum of Balinese life, coining phrases such as "Lanai lovelies" and "aman wannabes". *Taman Bebek*, the "Duck Garden" perched on the edge of a mountain slope in central Ubud, is Made Wijaya's solution for visitors in search of a home stay. Surrounded by a traditional tropical Balinese garden that plunges steeply into the Ayung River, Taman Bebek's combination of comfort and rustic ease stretches to six individual villas and a luxury suite. It is an easygoing family place and, rather like a family story, it has "grown and grown" since the first seeds were planted in 1984.

Made Wijaya, alias Michael White, stammt aus Australien, doch er gehört seit den 1970er Jahren so selbstverständlich zu Bali wie Reisfelder und Dorfschreine. Als Gebäude- und Landschaftsarchitekt, Tennislehrer, vor allem aber als unverbesserlicher Chronist der Geschehnisse im kosmopolitischen Bali ist er auf der Insel ebenso beliebt wie berüchtigt.

In zahlreichen Reportagen und Büchern beschrieb Wijaya ein breites Spektrum balinesischen Lebens und prägte unvergessliche Wortschöpfungen wie diese: »Lanai lovelies« oder »aman wannabes«. *Taman Bebek* – »Entengarten« – duckt sich an den Rand eines Berghangs in Zentral-Ubud. Hier empfängt Made Wijaya Gäste, die sich wie zu Hause fühlen möchten. Um Taman Bebeks sechs individuell eingerichtete Villen und eine Luxussuite wächst ein traditioneller tropischer Garten, der steil in den Fluss Ayung abfällt. Familien fühlen sich hier wohl, und wie eine Familie ist die Anlage gewachsen und gewachsen, seit die ersten Samen 1984 gepflanzt wurden.

Depuis le milieu des années 1970, l'Australien Michael White, alias Made Wijaya, fait partie du paysage balinais au même titre que les rizières ou les sanctuaires villageois. Architecte, paysagiste, entraîneur de tennis et, avant tout, chroniqueur invétéré de la vie cosmopolite à Bali, il est à la fois la mouche du coche et l'enfant chéri de l'île.

Dans une kyrielle d'articles et de livres, il a brossé un tableau de la vie balinaise, forgeant des expressions telles que «lanai lovelies» (mignonnes de véranda) et «aman wannabes». *Taman Bebek*, le «Jardin des Canards», sur le versant d'une montagne d'Ubud, au centre de Bali, s'adresse aux visiteurs qui aiment se sentir chez eux en voyage. Au beau milieu d'un jardin tropical balinais traditionnel qui descend à pic jusqu'à l'Ayung, le mélange de confort et d'aisance rustique de Taman Bebek se retrouve dans six villas et une suite de luxe. C'est un endroit décontracté, une sorte d'histoire familiale qui n'a cessé de se développer depuis que les premières graines en ont été semées en 1984.

❀ **PREVIOUS PAGES** A water jar in a lush Balinese garden overlooks views of paddy fields and mountains. **ABOVE ANS FACING PAGE** private balconies in Taman Bebek's villas. ❀ **VORHERGEHENDE DOPPELSEITE** ein Wassertrog in dem üppigen balinesischen Garten, Blick auf Reisfelder und Berge. **OBEN** private Balkone in den Villen von Taman Bebek. ❀ **DOUBLE PAGE PRECEDENTE** un baquet rempli d'eau dans le jardin luxuriant, sur arrière-plan de rizières et de montagnes. **CI-DESSUS** le balcon privé d'une des villas.

138 TAMAN BEBEK INDONESIA

❋ **ABOVE** An infinity edged swimming pool follows the contours of terraced rice fields in Taman Bebek's tiered garden. ❋ **OBEN** Ein Swimmingpool zeichnet in seinen freien Formen die Konturen terrassenförmig angelegter Reisfelder in dem stufenweise gestalteten Garten Taman Bebeks nach. ❋ **CI-DESSUS** Une piscine épouse les contours des rizières dans le jardin en terrasses de Taman Bebek.

❋ **RIGHT AND BELOW** colonial teak furniture on the verandas of Taman Bebek's villas. The double roof in tiles and thatch is typically Balinese. **FACING PAGE** Louvred teak doors and windows lead from the veranda to the bedroom. Patterned woodwork in teak and bamboo helps the circulation of fresh air. ❋ **RECHTS UND UNTEN** Teakmöbel im Kolonialstil auf den Veranden der Villen von Taman Bebek. Das doppelte Dach aus Ziegeln und Stroh ist typisch für Bali. **RECHTE SEITE** Jalousietüren aus Teak führen von der Veranda ins Schlafzimmer. Durch die gemusterten Holzeinbauten aus Teak und Bambus zieht stetig frische Luft. ❋ **A DROITE ET CI-DESSOUS** Les vérandas des villas sont équipées de meubles coloniaux en teck. Le toit double en chaume et tuile est typiquement balinais. **PAGE DE DROITE** Des portes et des fenêtres à claire-voie en teck séparent la véranda de la chambre. Des boiseries en teck et bambou laissent circuler l'air frais.

Taman Selini

Singaraja Bali

A hidden idyll for lotus eaters.

Nothern Bali is not where the crowds go. It is much the lesser known and unspoilt part of Bali, far from the crowded beaches, bars and boutiques of Kuta and Sanur. In fact, it is a three-hour drive from "Bali buzz", the strips that give the island its faint air of adrenalin rush and notoriety.

Up north, another Bali exists in traditional fishing villages such as Pemuteran, where a slower pace and quieter life exalt the atmosphere of bril liant skies reflected in waters of sparkling clarity. At night the sky is strewn with stars like fireflies. Appropriately, *Taman Selini* means "The Garden of the Moon". Its eleven hideaway bungalows are reached after a drive lined with tamarind trees. Owned and run by a Greek-Balinese family, the bungalows were built using local materials and artisans, and local villagers were trained for employment. Every bungalow boasts its own private garden and open-air shower. Luxuriantly planted with bougainvillea, jacaranda, frangipani and japonica, the property melts into the nearby hills, the West Bali National Reserve, which abounds with bird and wildlife. Hidden Bali exists; it still has seasons and reasons.

Die Massen zieht es nicht nach Nordbali, den weniger bekannten und unberührteren Teil der Insel, der von den überfüllten Stränden, Bars und Boutiquen von Kuta und Sanur weit entfernt liegt. Drei Stunden fährt man vom »Bali buzz«, den Pisten, deren Ruf von Adrenalinschüben und traurigen Berühmtheiten bestimmt wird.

Weiter nördlich findet man ein anderes Bali mit traditionellen Fischerdörfern wie Pemuteran, wo man das Leben ruhiger und gelassener angeht, im Einklang mit dem strahlend blauen Himmel, der sich im glasklaren Wasser spiegelt. Nachts ist der Himmel voller Sterne, und passenderweise bedeutet *Taman Selini* »Mondgarten«. Mit dem Auto gelangt man über eine mit Tamarinden gesäumte Straße zu den elf versteckten Bungalows, die von einheimischen Handwerkern mit dort vorhandenem Baumaterial errichtet wurden. Die griechisch-balinesische Familie, die die Anlage betreibt, wählte auch ihr Personal unter den Einheimischen. Alle Bungalows verfügen über einen eigenen Garten und eine Außendusche. Die Anlage, die verschwenderisch mit Bougainvillea, Jakaranda- und Pagodenbäumen, sowie mit Japanischer Quitte bepflanzt wurde, geht nahtlos in die angrenzenden Hügel über. Dort liegt das »West Bali National Reserve«, ein Naturschutzgebiet mit zahlreichen wilden Tieren und vielen Vögeln.

Le nord de Bali n'est pas un endroit où les foules se pressent. Cette région encore intacte est la moins connue de l'île : elle est loin des plages bondées, des bars, boutiques et stripteases de Kuta et Sanur qui font la notoriété de Bali.

A trois heures de route au nord de la «rumeur balinaise», on découvre l'autre face de l'île, dans des villages traditionnels de pêcheurs comme Pemuteran, où la lenteur et le calme exaltent le ciel d'un bleu éclatant qui se reflète dans des eaux cristallines. La nuit, les étoiles innombrables brillent comme des lucioles. C'est fort à propos que *Taman Selini*, le «Jardin de la lune», porte son nom. Ce complexe de onze bungalows retirés au bout d'un chemin bordé de tamarins est la propriété d'une famille gréco-balinaise qui en assure la direction. Les bungalows ont été construits dans des matériaux locaux par des artisans du village. Le personnel a aussi été recruté sur place. Chaque bungalow dispose d'un jardin et d'une douche en plein air. Avec sa végétation luxuriante de bougainvilliers, jacarandas, frangipaniers et cognassiers du Japon, la propriété se fond dans les collines environnantes, la West Bali National Reserve, un parc naturel protégé où abondent les oiseaux et les animaux sauvages. La Bali secrète existe ; elle a encore ses saisons et ses raisons.

※ **FACING PAGE** The pool is set against a backdrop of wooded hills. **FACING PAGE BOTTOM AND ABOVE** Taman Selini's hospitality extends to a private beach and a deep blue sea. **FOLLOWING PAGES** Each tastefully decorated bungalow opens on to a private veranda and landscaped gardens. ※ **LINKE SEITE OBEN** der Swimmingpool vor dem Hintergrund bewaldeter Hügel. **LINKE SEITE UNTEN UND OBEN** Die Anlage bietet auch einen Privatstrand am dunkelblauen Meer. **FOLGENDE DOPPELSEITE** Alle Bungalows sind geschmackvoll eingerichtet und führen auf eine private Terrasse und eine gepflegte Gartenanlage hinaus. ※ **PAGE DE GAUCHE, EN HAUT** la piscine, avec en toile de fond, des collines boisées. **PAGE DE GAUCHE, EN BAS ET CI-DESSUS** Taman Selini offre aussi une plage privée en bordure de la mer d'encre. **DOUBLE PAGE SUIVANTE** Tous les bungalows, décorés avec goût, donnent sur une véranda privée et des jardins paysagés.

Vista Linda

The Feng Shui House

Tony Gonzales and Tes Pasola

Cala Perdida

Toni and Mari Escano

Tony and Margie Floirendo

PHILIPPINES

Vista Linda
Quezon City

A house insoired by the sunrise.

Years ago, when the house was originally built for a doctor in ornate Spanish colonial style, the Mexican ambassador came visiting. Looking at the view over Marikina Valley he remarked: "Que vista moy linda est!" (What a lovely view).

The property has been called Vista Linda ever since, even though the present house is an extensive renovation undertaken by its new owners, a lawyer with a passion for collecting vintage sports cars and his wife, who is a writer. Both are avowed modernists who have long admired the stark spaces and empty courtyards of Luis Barragan. They approached Ed Calma, the innovative Filipino architect, to reconfigure the house completely. Vista Linda's fourteen bedrooms were reduced to half the number; the roofline was changed and high ceilings were introduced. Plain walls, stone floors and functional interiors now give on to simple gardens. "The house has imposed upon us a discipline against accumulating things," says the writer. But it is the perfect setting for the lawyer's ten vintage cars.

Als der mexikanische Botschafter vor vielen Jahren in dem Haus zu Besuch war, das ursprünglich für einen Arzt prunkvoll im spanischen Kolonialstil eingerichtet worden war, sagte er über die Aussicht auf das Marikina-Tal: »Que vista moy linda est!« (Was für ein schöner Ausblick).

Seitdem wird das Anwesen Vista Linda genannt, obwohl die neuen Besitzer, ein Rechtsanwalt und leidenschaftlicher Sammler von alten Sportwagen, und seine Frau, eine Schriftstellerin, es aufwändig renoviert haben. Die beiden schwören auf die Moderne und bewunderten schon lange die schlichten Räume und leeren Innenhöfe des mexikanischen Architekten Luis Barragáns. Sie beauftragten den innovativen philippinischen Architekten Ed Calma, das Haus vollkommen neu zu gestalten. Er reduzierte die vierzehn Schlafzimmer des Vista Linda um die Hälfte, veränderte die Konturen des Dachs und baute die Räume höher. Nackte Wände, Steinböden und die funktionelle Einrichtung wurden mit schlicht gestalteten Gärten kombiniert. »Das Haus legt uns die Disziplin auf, nicht zu viele Dinge anzuhäufen«, erklärt die Schriftstellerin. Aber es gibt einen perfekten Hintergrund für die zehn alten Sportwagen des Rechtsanwalts ab.

Il y a des années, cette maison appartenait alors à un médecin qui l'avait fait construire dans un style colonial espagnol très ornementé, l'ambassadeur du Mexique en visite s'était exclamé en admirant la vue sur la vallée de Marikina : «Que vista moy linda es!» (Quelle belle vue !)

La propriété a gardé ce nom de Vista Linda, bien que ses nouveaux propriétaires, un avocat passionné de voitures de sport anciennes et sa femme, écrivain, aient rénové la maison de fond en comble. Ces modernistes déclarés admiraient de longue date les espaces austères et les cours dépouillées de Luis Barragán. Ils ont chargé Ed Calma, un architecte philippin novateur, de remodeler entièrement les lieux. Il ne reste que sept chambres des 14 chambres d'origine ; la ligne de toit a été modifiée et les plafonds relevés. Un intérieur fonctionnel aux murs sobres et aux sols en pierre donne désormais sur des jardins agencés sans sophistication. «La maison nous astreint à ne pas accumuler les objets», dit l'écrivain. Mais c'est l'endroit rêvé pour exposer les dix voitures de collection de l'avocat.

✳ **ABOVE** Instead of a conventional entrance with a gate, architect Ed Calma created an open plaza with an accent provided by a yellow metal sculpture by his architect father, Lor Calma. ✳ **OBEN** Statt des üblichen Toreingangs schuf der Architekt Ed Calma eine offene Plaza mit einer gelben Metallskulptur seines Vaters Lor Calma. ✳ **CI-DESSUS** Plutôt qu'une entrée traditionnelle avec portail, l'architecte Ed Calma a créé un espace ouvert auquel une sculpture jaune en métal donne du relief. Il d'agit d'une œuvre de son père, l'architecte Lor Calma.

❋ **ABOVE** A small brook with a slate bridge separates the ten-car garage from the garden. The car is a Lotus Elise. **FOLLOWING PAGES, CLOCKWISE FROM TOP LEFT** Stairs lead to the bedrooms above. In the living room, the lounge chairs by Le Corbusier, side table by Eileen Grey and baby grand piano in black blend with the floor. The master bedroom has a private balcony and maple hardwood floor. Frosted glass partitions separate the guest rooms from the library. The chaise longue is by Le Corbusier. ❋ **OBEN** Ein kleiner Bach mit einer Schieferbrücke trennt den Garten von der Garage für die zehn Sportwagen. Das gelbe Auto ist ein Lotus Elise. **FOLGENDE DOPPELSEITE, IM UHRZEIGERSINN VON LINKS OBEN** Die Treppe führt zu den Schlafzimmern im ersten Stock. Im Wohnzimmer passen die Sessel von Le Corbusier, der Beistelltisch von Eileen Grey und der schwarze Stutzflügel gut zu dem dunklen Boden. Das große Schlafzimmer wurde mit einem Balkon und Ahorn-Hartholzparkett versehen. Trennwände aus Milchglas verwehren die Sicht von der Bibliothek auf die Gästezimmer. Die Liege ist ebenfalls von Le Corbusier. ❋ **CI-DESSUS** Un ruisseau qu'enjambe un pont en ardoise sépare le jardin du garage qui abrite les dix voitures de collection. La voiture jaune est une Lotus Elise. **DOUBLE PAGE SUIVANTE, DANS LE SENS DES AIGUILLES D'UNE MONTRE, À PARTIR D'EN HAUT À GAUCHE** l'escalier qui mène aux chambres à coucher de l'étage supérieur. Dans le salon, des fauteuils Le Corbusier, une desserte d'Eileen Grey et un piano demi-queue noir se marient parfaitement avec le sol. La chambre de maîtres est dotée d'un parquet en érable et d'un balcon. Des panneaux en verre sablé séparent les pièces de réception de la bibliothèque. La chaise longue est signée Le Corbusier.

THE Feng SHUi HOUSE

MANiLA

Floating life energies thanks to Feng Shui.

The young and worldly scion of an old Chinese family in Manila was married not long ago. Well before the impending nuptials, he commissioned Filipino architect and designer Ramon Antonio to design a large family home in one of Manila's well-heeled residential districts.

The brief was specific: a bright new look, plenty of cross ventilation, views into the garden and the sound of running water. Many of the requests demanded an adherence to the principles of Feng Shui. The ancient Chinese practice of directing the flow of good energy decrees that a main door should not directly open into the living room. Antonio created a floating wall at the main entrance to create a small art gallery. Neutral colours, the use of water bodies, the placement of bedrooms according to birth signs of occupants, even the position of the stove in the kitchen, were dictated by Feng Shui. The uninformed visitor may be impervious to the powers of the Feng Shui house. But he will carry back an impression of elements – light, air, earth and water – mingling in harmony.

Der junge, weltmännische Spross einer alten chinesischen Familie in Manila hat sich jüngst vermählt. Lange vor der geplanten Hochzeitsfeier beauftragte er den philippinischen Architekten und Designer Ramon Antonio mit dem Bau eines großen Einfamilienhauses in einem wohlhabenden Wohngebiet Manilas.

Die Vorgaben waren klar: ein strahlend neuer Look, reichlich Querlüftung, Ausblicke in den Garten und der Klang fließenden Wassers. Viele dieser Forderungen waren an den Prinzipien des Feng Shui ausgerichtet. Die alte chinesische Methode, die Lebensenergie ungehindert fließen zu lassen, erfordert, dass vom Hauseingang keine Tür direkt ins Wohnzimmer führt. Antonio entwarf am Haupteingang eine wie schwebend vorgesetzte Wand für eine kleine Kunstgalerie. Neutrale Farben, eingebaute Wasserbecken, die Anordnung der Schlafzimmer entsprechend den Geburtszeichen der Bewohner, ja sogar die Stelle, wo der Ofen in der Küche stehen durfte – alles war von Feng Shui bestimmt. Unwissenden Besuchern bleiben die Prinzipien des Feng-Shui-Hauses vielleicht verschlossen, aber auch sie spüren, dass sich hier die Elemente Licht, Luft, Erde und Wasser in Harmonie befinden.

Cet homme du monde, jeune descendant d'une vieille famille chinoise de Manille, s'est marié récemment. Mais bien avant la date prévue pour les noces, il avait chargé l'architecte et designer philippin Ramon Antonio de concevoir une grande maison individuelle dans l'un des quartiers huppés de la ville.

Le programme était précis : look flambant neuf, de multiples ventilations transversales, vue sur le jardin et murmure de l'eau. Nombre de ces points exigeaient la mise en application de principes du Feng Shui. Selon cette pratique chinoise ancienne visant à canaliser les flux d'énergies positives, une porte d'entrée ne doit pas s'ouvrir directement sur le salon. C'est pourquoi l'architecte a imaginé une cloison suspendue qui tient aussi lieu de petite galerie d'art. Les couleurs neutres, les bassins et la distribution des chambres en fonction du signe de naissance de leurs occupants, voire l'emplacement du fourneau dans la cuisine, se conforment aussi aux règles du Feng Shui. Le visiteur non averti peut rester indifférent aux pouvoirs de la maison Feng Shui ; il en emportera cependant une impression de mariage harmonieux des quatre éléments.

✳ **ABOVE** The living room, overlooking the southeast, is filled with light. The furniture is upholstered in Jim Thompson fabric. **BELOW** The floating wall is dictated by Feng Shui principles. The cantilevered console displays saddle fragments from Maranaw province. The circular painting is by Filipino artist Gus Albor. ✳ **OBEN** Das nach Südosten ausgerichtete Wohnzimmer ist sehr hell. Die Möbel sind mit Jim-Thompson-Stoffen bezogen. **UNTEN** Feng-Shui-Prinzipien erfordern die wie schwebend vorgesetzte Wand, davor steht ein freistehender Konsoltisch, auf dem Sattelteile aus der Provinz Maranaw ausgestellt sind. Das runde Gemälde hat der philippinische Künstler Gus Albor gemalt. ✳ **CI-DESSOUS** Le salon exposé sud-est est inondé de lumière. Les sièges sont recouverts de tissus Jim Thompson. **CI-DESSOUS** La cloison suspendue est dictée par des principes du Feng Shui. Sur la console suspendue sont exposés des fragments de selles provenant de la province de Maranaw. Le tableau circulaire a été peint par l'artiste philippin Gus Albor.

※ **ABOVE** Handloom silk blinds in the living room were made in Manila. The Cubist oil paintings are by prominent Filipino artist Arturo Luz. A circular chrome drop light lends contrast to the natural textures of the room. **BELOW** Antique porcelain and lacquer objects from China and Myanmar counterpoint the sectional sofas made by the Italian firm Minotti. ※ **OBEN** Die handgewebten Seidenrollos im Wohnzimmer wurden in Manila angefertigt. Die kubistisch anmutenden Ölgemälde sind von dem bekannten philippinischen Künstler Arturo Luz. Eine runde Hängelampe aus Chrom kontrastiert mit den sonst natürlichen Materialien im Raum. **UNTEN** Antike chinesische und burmesische Kunstwerke aus Porzellan und Lack bilden einen Kontrapunkt zu den Anbausofas der italienischen Firma Minotti. ※ **CI-DESSUS** Les stores en soie tissés à la main du salon ont été réalisés à Manille. Les peintures à l'huile cubistes sont d'Arturo Luz, un artiste philippin en vue. Une suspension circulaire chromée attire le regard au milieu des matières naturelles. **CI-DESSOUS** Des objets d'art anciens en porcelaine et en laque provenant de Birmanie et de Chine contrastent élégamment avec les sofas modulaires de la société italienne Minotti.

TONY GONZALES AND TES PASOLA

MANILA

An expression of a dynamic spirit.

Two talented young designers, who specialize in making furniture, stationery and giftware, acquired a 459 sq. meter plot in Manila and wanted a house with a difference to share with their small son Tymone.

There wasn't the slightest doubt in their minds as to who could create it for them: only their friend Budji Layug, one of the most respected names in Asian design. Layug has created a three-story residence of clean lines, vaunting height emphasized by a slanting roof and enough glass to create the feeling of a cathedral. A dramatic innovation in the Gonzales-Pasola home is Layug's cantilevered staircase that becomes a sculptural feature of the living room. Another is the sleight of hand by which the tropical outdoors is brought inside: glass extensions and balconies conspire to reflect the lush foliage and cobalt-tiled pool of the garden. Everywhere are displayed objects, designed either by the owners or one of their artist friends, that vividly convey the exuberant spirit of contemporary Filipino style.

Zwei junge talentierte, auf Möbel, Schreibwaren und Geschenkartikel spezialisierte Designer kauften ein 459 Quadratmeter großes Grundstück in Manila und planten für sich und ihren kleinen Sohn Tymone ein Haus mit dem gewissen Etwas.

Sie kannten nur einen, der dafür infrage kam: ihr gemeinsamer Freund Budji Layug – ein in Asien sehr geschätzter Designer. Layug hat eine dreistöckige Villa mit klaren Linien entworfen, dessen enorme Höhe durch ein schräges Dach noch betont wird sowie durch genügend Glas, um sie wie eine Kathedrale wirken zu lassen. Layugs freitragende Treppe wirkt im Wohnzimmer der Gonzales-Pasola wie ein bildhauerisches Element. Auch die tropische Außenwelt wurde geschickt nach innen verlagert: Anbauten aus Glas und mehrere Balkone sorgen dafür, dass sich die üppigen Blätter und das Kobaltblau der Poolfliesen dort spiegeln. Überall sind Ausstellungsstücke verstreut, die entweder von den Eigentümern selbst stammen oder von einem ihrer Künstlerfreunde, die den markanten Stil des zeitgenössischen philippinischen Designs beispielhaft zum Ausdruck bringen.

Deux jeunes designers talentueux, spécialisés dans la création de mobilier, d'articles de papeterie et de cadeaux, avaient fait l'acquisition d'un terrain de 459 m² à Manille et voulaient pour eux et leur jeune fils Tymone une maison pas comme les autres.

Pour eux, il ne faisait pas l'ombre d'un doute qu'une seule personne était à la hauteur de cette tâche : leur ami Budji Layug, un grand nom de l'architecture en Asie. Aussi Layug a-t-il conçu une villa à trois étages aux lignes épurées, d'une belle hauteur accentuée par une toiture pentue et des baies vitrées, le tout donnant à cette maison une allure de cathédrale. L'escalier suspendu du salon fait l'effet d'une sculpture. On remarque aussi la subtilité avec laquelle le monde tropical extérieur est présent à l'intérieur : des extensions vitrées et des balcons reflètent la végétation luxuriante et le carrelage bleu cobalt de la piscine. Les objets exposés dans toutes les pièces, œuvres des propriétaires eux-mêmes ou d'artistes auxquels ils sont liés, traduisent de manière éloquente l'exubérance du style philippin contemporain.

❀ **FACING PAGE** The "Cocoon" lounge chair of welded wire is by Filippino artist Ann Pamintuan. The sofas and coffee table of woven abaca are by furniture designer Milo Naval. **ABOVE** The vase of recycled paper is by Tes Pasola. ❀ **LINKE SEITE** Der »Cocoon« Lounge-Sessel aus geschweißtem Draht stammt von der philippinischen Künstlerin Ann Pamintuan. Der Möbeldesigner Milo Naval entwarf die Sofas und den Couchtisch aus geflochtenem Manilahanf. **OBEN** Die Vase aus recyceltem Papier stammt von Tes Pasola. ❀ **PAGE DE GAUCHE** L'artiste philippine Ann Pamintuan a imaginé le fauteuil « Cocoon », en fils de fer soudés. Les canapés et la table basse en fibre d'abaca tressée sont signés Milo Naval. **EN HAUT** Le vase en papier recyclé est de Tes Pasola.

TONI AND MARI
ESCANO
MANILA

Asian fusion fully alive.

Toni and Mari Escano's ample home, with its shady verandas and palm-filled gardens in a quiet suburb of Metro Manila, is a fine family home: the bustle of their five children or the patter of beloved dogs is never far away.

A collaboration between architect Emmanuel Enriquez and interior designer Budji Layug, the house has the classic look of a style acknowledged as Asian fusion. Traditional artifacts – old Indonesian doors, Filipino pottery, Tibetan prayer stones – are combined with examples of modern art and contemporary creations in wood, rattan, leather, metal, silk and cotton. The living space, with its six meter-high ceiling, is lofty; light filters in through the two-story house through stands of bamboo and pocket-sized tropical pebble gardens, unexpectedly tucked in at the sides. The Escanos are sometimes surprised by the contradictory impulses that inspired their eclectic home and collection. But they are always delighted to hear that it makes for a warm, easy and comfortable fit.

Toni und Mari Escanos weitläufiges Haus mit den schattigen Terrassen und vielen Palmen in den Gärten liegt in einem ruhigen Vorort von Manila. Aber im Haus selbst tobt das Familienleben: Die fünf Kinder und ihre geliebten Hunde sind meistens nicht zu überhören.

Das Haus ist ein Gemeinschaftswerk des Architekten Emmanuel Enriquez und des Innenarchitekten Budji Layug, die es in einem Stil eingerichtet haben, den man als Asian Fusion bezeichnet. Traditionelle Artefakte – alte indonesische Türen, philippinische Tonwaren, tibetische Gebetssteine – werden mit Elementen der modernen Kunst und zeitgenössischen Kreationen aus Holz, Rattan, Leder, Metall, Seide und Baumwolle kombiniert. Der Wohnbereich wirkt mit seiner sechs Meter hohen Decke erlesen; in das zweistöckige Haus fällt Licht aus den unerwartetsten Quellen – durch Bambusstauden und kleine Kiesgärten im Westentaschenformat, die an allen Ecken angelegt sind. Manchmal staunen selbst die Escanos noch über die widersprüchlichen Impulse, die sie zu ihrem eklektizistischen Haus und der dazugehörigen Sammlung inspiriert haben. Sie freuen sich jedoch immer zu hören, was für eine warme, angenehme und gemütliche Ausstrahlung es hat.

Située dans une banlieue tranquille de Manille, la vaste et belle maison de Toni et Mari Escano résonne en permanence du trottinement de leur chien adoré et du joyeux vacarme de leurs cinq enfants.

Fruit de la collaboration entre l'architecte Emmanuel Enriquez et le décorateur Budji Layug, cette villa aux terrasses ombragées et au jardin envahi par les palmiers illustre bien le style appelé Asian fusion. Des objets traditionnels – portes indonésiennes anciennes, poterie philippine, pierres à prières tibétaines – sont combinés avec des œuvres d'art modernes et des créations contemporaines en bois, rotin, cuir, métal, soie et coton. Le séjour avec ses six mètres de hauteur sous plafond est aéré ; la lumière se glisse à l'intérieur de cette construction à deux étages en passant à travers des rideaux de bambou et les jardins tropicaux de la taille d'un mouchoir de poche dissimulés sur les côtés. Les Escano sont parfois surpris par les inspirations contradictoires perceptibles dans leur maison et sa décoration éclectique. Mais ils sont toujours ravis d'entendre que leur chez eux est chaleureux, confortable et agréable à vivre.

❄ **PREVIOUS PAGES** A profusion of stones, from antique grinding stones to Tibetan prayer stones, lie in corners of the courtyard and garden. **BELOW** The plant-filled entrance to the Escano home is a pair of old wooden doors. The L-shaped stone bench is topped by an antique Muslim burial marker. **FACING PAGE** in the foyer, an old chest from Ifugao province, topped by a modern mirror by Budji Layug. A towering ceremonial post in the centre of the living room which overlooks the bamboo-filled garden. ❄ **VORHERGEHENDE DOPPELSEITE** Im Innenhof und im Garten befinden sich zahlreiche Steine – von antiken Mahlsteinen bis zu tibetischen Gebetssteinen. **UNTEN** Der grün bepflanzte Eingangsbereich zum Anwesen der Escanos besteht aus antiken Holztüren. Auf der L-förmigen Steinbank steht ein antiker muslimischer Grabstein. **RECHTE SEITE** Im Eingangsbereich steht eine alte Kommode aus der philippinischen Provinz Ifugao. Darauf steht ein von Budji Layug entworfener moderner Spiegel. **UNTEN** Ein hoher Zeremonienpfahl steht mitten im Wohnzimmer, das auf den mit Bambus bepflanzten Garten hinausgeht. ❄ **DOUBLE PAGE PRECEDENTE** Une grande quantité de pierres – meules anciennes et pierres à prière tibétaines, entre autres – sont entreposées dans le jardin et la cour intérieure. **CI-DESSOUS** L'accès à la maison des Escano se fait par deux portes anciennes en bois perdues dans la verdure. Une ancienne pierre tombale musulmane est posée sur le banc de pierre. **PAGE DE DROITE** Dans l'entrée, une commode ancienne de la province d'Ifugao est surmontée d'un miroir moderne signé Budji Layug. Un mât de cérémonie domine le salon qui s'ouvre sur le jardin planté de bambous.

CALA PERDIDA
Batangas Province

A romantic interlude.

Calatagan is a finger of land in Batangas province that stretches into the South China Sea. A couple of hours south of Manila, it is a verdant land of sugarcane and corn plantations overlooking a spectacular beach.

Riding his motorbike in the area one cool morning Franco Delgado, a veteran of Manila's boardrooms, came upon a property that captured his heart. He pursued its acquisition like a besotted lover. From the start, Delgado had a vision of the shape his dream hideout would take: wholly Asian in form and spirit, it had to blend effortlessly with the landscape. The result is a highly individual two-story structure of pillared verandas and wraparound decks topped with an imposing thatched roof. The prominent arch of the roof was borrowed from rustic rice barns known locally as *lumbung*. Delgado has resisted landscaping his rural retreat – he just cleaned it up, snipping off a few branches here and there. To complete his love story he has romantically named it Cala Perdida – Lost Cove.

Calatagan in der Provinz Batangas erstreckt sich als Landzunge ins Südchinesische Meer. Die grüne, von Zuckerrohr und Getreidefeldern geprägte Landschaft liegt nur wenige Autostunden südlich von Manila an einem wunderschönen Strand.

Eines kühlen Morgens, als er mit dem Motorrad durch die Gegend fuhr, entdeckte Franco Delgado, der seit langen Jahren in den verschiedensten Unternehmen Manilas eine leitende Position einnimmt, ein Anwesen, in das er sich auf der Stelle verliebte. Mit der Energie eines Frischverliebten sah er zu, dass er bekam, was er wollte. Von Anfang an wusste Delgado, wie sein Traumversteck aussehen sollte: Von oben bis unten asiatisch in Geist und Gestalt und eins mit der Landschaft. Das zweistöckige Gebäude mit einer säulengeschmückten Terrasse und einem rundherum gebauten Balkon wird von einem mächtigen Strohdach gekrönt. Das auffällig gebogene Dach wurde in seiner Form an die traditionellen, lokalen Reisscheunen, den *lumbung*, angelehnt. Delgado verzichtete darauf, die Landschaft um seine ländliche Zufluchtsstätte herum zu gestalten. Hier und da ließ er ein paar Äste abschneiden und das Erscheinungsbild geringfügig bereinigen. Zum Happy End dieser Liebesgeschichte nannte er das Haus Cala Perdida: Verlorene Bucht.

Calatagan, dans la province de Batangas, est une langue de terre qui avance dans la mer de Chine méridionale. A quelques heures de route au sud de Manille, surplombant une superbe plage, on découvre un paysage verdoyant de plantations de canne à sucre et de céréales.

C'est à l'occasion d'une sortie en moto par une fraîche matinée que Franco Delgado, vétéran des conseils d'administration de Manille, a eu le coup de foudre pour cette propriété. Avec l'énergie que donne la passion, il a tout fait pour l'acquérir. Il avait dès le départ une idée précise de la planque de ses rêves : entièrement asiatique dans sa forme et son esprit, elle devait se fondre sans effort dans le paysage. Le résultat : une construction originale de deux étages, dotée d'une terrasse à colonnades et d'un balcon sur ses quatre côtés, coiffée d'un imposant toit de chaume. Ce toit en carène est un emprunt à l'architecture régionale des *lumbung* (greniers à riz). Delgado a renoncé à remodeler l'environnement de son refuge, se contentant de faire un grand nettoyage et de scier quelques branches ça et là. Pour parachever cette histoire d'amour, il a donné à sa maison le nom romantique de Cala Perdida, «Crique perdue».

❋ **FACING PAGE** The outer walls of the house are lined with woven bamboo matting. The wooden chairs on the upper deck are from Ifugao province. **ABOVE** A wide stairway links the lower and upper decks of the house. The thatched roof with its pointed arch was inspired by local rice barns known as *lumbung*. **FOLLOWING PAGES** The interiors are decorated with artifacts from Ifugao, woven bamboo walls and bamboo blinds. ❋ **LINKE SEITE** Die Außenwände sind mit geflochtenen Bambusmatten verkleidet. Die Holzstühle auf dem oberen Balkon stammen aus der Provinz Ifugao. **OBEN** Eine breite Treppe verbindet die untere Terrasse mit dem Balkon. Das spitz zulaufende Strohdach wurde von den Reisscheunen, den *lumbung*, inspiriert. **FOLGENDE DOPPELSEITE** Die Räume sind mit Objekten aus Ifugao, geflochtenen Bambusmatten an den Wänden und Bambusjalousien eingerichtet. ❋ **PAGE DE GAUCHE** Les murs extérieurs de la maison sont doublés de sparterie en bambou. **CI-DESSOUS** Les chaises en bois sur le balcon proviennent de la province d'Ifugao. **CI-DESSUS** Un large escalier relie la terrasse au balcon. Le toit de chaume en carène est inspiré des *lumbung*, les silos à riz de la région. **DOUBLE PAGE SUIVANTE** Des objets d'Ifugao, des sparteries et des stores de bambou décorent les pièces.

Malipano Island Mindanao

The sun adds lustre to a pearl farm.

Off the coast of the southern province of Mindanao, in secluded coves blessed with white sandy beaches, is a private retreat on the tiny island of Malipano.

Once a pearl farm where thousands of oysters were cultured for white, pink and champagne pearls, it is the home of Tony and Margie Floirendo, who inherited the property from his father Antonio, the banana king of the Philippines. Tony is a politician who represents the district in the national legislature; Margie was Miss Universe in 1973. Adapted from the dwellings of indigenous tribes, architect Fancisco Manosa built three structures on stilts over the water. The octagonal rooftops, made of bamboo shingles, derive from the shape of a local farmer's gourd hat. In keeping with the Floirendos' wish, only local materials were used: wood for floors and limestone for the walkways. Landscape designer Ponce Veridiano planted the gardens. From the veranda, the oceanic panorama and the sun setting over Mount Apo, the highest peak in the Philippines, can be a humbling experience.

Auf der kleinen Insel Malipano vor der Küste der südlichen Provinz Mindanao liegt umgeben von kleinen Buchten mit weißem Sandstrand ein privates Strandhaus.

Früher stand hier das Haus eines Perlenzüchters, der tausende von Austern wegen der weißen, rosaund champagnerfarbenen Perlen züchtete. Nun leben Tony und Margie Floirendo hier. Tony erbte das Anwesen von seinem Vater Antonio, dem »Bananenkönig« der Philippinen. Er selbst vertritt den Bezirk als Abgeordneter im Parlament, während Margie 1973 zur Miss Universe gekürt wurde. Der Architekt Francisco Manosa baute direkt über dem Wasser drei Pfahlbauten und griff damit die Bauweise der einheimischen Häuser auf. Auch die achteckigen Dächer aus Bambusziegeln beziehen sich auf die Flaschenkürbisform der traditionellen Bauernhütten. Entsprechend dem Wunsch der Floirendos wurde nur natürliches Baumaterial verwendet, so sind die Böden aus Holz und die Fußwege aus Kalkstein. Der Landschaftsarchitekt Ponce Veridiano gestaltete die üppigen Gärten. Der Blick von der Veranda auf den Ozean und den Sonnenuntergang über dem Berg Apo, dem höchsten Gipfel der Philippinen, kann den Betrachter demütig stimmen.

Une maison de plage s'élève sur l'îlot de Malipano, au large des côtes de la province méridionale de Mindanao, entourée de criques abritant des plages de sable blanc.

Tony Floirendo a hérité de son père Antonio, banana king des Philippines, cette ancienne exploitation où l'on a autrefois élevé des milliers d'huîtres pour leurs perles blanches, rosées ou champagne. Tony, député à l'assemblée nationale, et son épouse margie, Miss Univers 1973, y ont élu domicile. S'inspirant de l'habitat indigène, l'architecte Francisco Manosa a construit trois corps de bâtiment sur pilotis au-dessus de l'eau. Les toits octogonaux en bardeaux de bambou sont des références aux huttes en forme de calebasse des paysans de la région. Pour répondre aux désirs du couple, on n'a utilisé que des matériaux locaux : bois au sol et pierre calcaire pour les sentiers. L'architecte paysagiste Ponce Veridiano a créé les jardins luxuriants. Regarder de la terrasse l'océan et le soleil se coucher sur le mont Apo, le point culminant des Philippines, est une leçon d'humilité.

※ **PREVIOUS PAGES** The Floirendo residence is composed of several structures on stilts, topped by bamboo shingle roofs. **ABOVE** the entrance to the residential area of the private island, made of solid, wooden slabs. A brass gong announces visitors. **FACING PAGE** The boat landing on the island. **FOLLOWING PAGES** The living room with open sea views has comfortable bamboo furniture. ※ **VORHERGEHENDE DOPPELSEITE** Das Anwesen der Floirendos besteht aus mehreren Pfahlbauten mit Dächern aus Bambusziegeln. **OBEN** Der Eingang zur Anlage auf der Privatinsel besteht aus festen Holzstufen. Ein Messinggong kündigt die Besucher an. **RECHTE SEITE** der Bootssteg der Insel. **FOLGENDE DOPPELSEITE** Bambusmöbel im Wohnzimmer mit Blick aufs offene Meer. ※ **DOUBLE PAGE PRECEDENTE** La résidence des Floirendo est composée de plusieurs corps de bâtiments sur pilotis et coiffés de toitures en bardeaux de bambou. **CI-DESSUS** Avec ses énormes pièces de bois, l'entrée de la partie habitation de cette île privée donne une impression massive. Les visiteurs s'annoncent en frappant sur le gong en laiton. **PAGE DE DROITE** lieu de mouillage des bateaux venant à l'île. **DOUBLE PAGE SUIVANTE** Le salon, qui jouit d'une vue dégagée sur la mer, est doté de meubles de bambou confortables.

The Forbidden Purple City

A Former Mandarin's H

vietnam

The Temple
of Princess Ngoc Son

Tran Quoc Pagoda

Garden House
on the Perfume River

The Hoi-An Bridge

THE FORBIDDEN PURPLE CITY

HUé

Ghostly echoes of China's Forbidden City.

In 1802 Nguyen Anh proclaimed himself the Emperor Gia Long and moved the imperial capital from Hanoi to Hué on the northern bank of the Perfume River. He embarked on a vast building programme and consulted geomancers to establish a new citadel.

A ten-kilometre long moat was dug for the complex and at its centre was the emperor's private palace, the Forbidden Purple City, inspired by the seat of the emperor of China. The network of palaces, gates and courtyards served as Gia Long's home and administrative core though the city suffered periodic damage from termites and typhoons. By the time Bao Dai, the last emperor, abdicated in 1945, the Forbidden Purple City had acquired dozens of pavilions and hundreds of rooms. All that changed in 1968 when American forces, in response to the communist takeover of Hué, blasted the city. Rice fields now cover much of what was once a sprawling royal complex. Only a handful of buildings remain but they give a clear sense of how the Vietnamese interpreted imperial Chinese architecture.

Im Jahre 1802 ernannte Nguyen Anh sich selbst zum Kaiser Gia Long und verlegte die kaiserliche Hauptstadt von Hanoi nach Hué am Nordufer des Parfümflusses. Er legte den Grundstein zu umfassenden Bautätigkeiten und konsultierte Geomanten, die die Lage der neuen Zitadelle auswählten.

Im Zentrum der neuen Palastanlage, die von einem zehn Kilometer langer Wassergraben umgeben war, lagen die Privatgemächer des Kaisers. Diese »Verbotene Purpurne Stadt« erinnert an den Sitz des Kaisers von China. In dieser Anlage mit Palästen, Toren und Höfen lebte Kaiser Gia Long und verwaltete von hier aus die Belange seiner Untertanen, obwohl die Stadt mehrfach unter Termiten und Taifunen litt. Als der letzte Kaiser Bao Dai 1945 abdankte, war die Verbotene Stadt auf dutzende von Pavillons mit hunderten von Räumen angewachsen. Nachdem die Kommunisten 1968 die Stadt eingenommen hatten, verwandelten die Amerikaner Hué in ein Trümmerfeld, und so bedecken heute Reisfelder ein großes Gebiet der einst so ausgedehnten Palastanlage. Nur wenige alte Gebäude blieben erhalten und bezeugen bis heute, wie die Vietnamesen die kaiserliche Architektur der Chinesen interpretierten.

En 1802, Nguyên Anh s'est proclamé empereur sous le nom de Gia Long et a transféré la capitale impériale de Hanoi à Hué, sur la rive gauche de la Rivière aux parfums. Gia Long s'est alors attelé à un vaste programme de construction, recourant aux services de géomanciens pour choisir l'emplacement d'une nouvelle citadelle.

Dix kilomètres de douves enserrent l'ensemble architectural au centre duquel se trouve la Cité pourpre interdite, réplique de la Cité interdite des empereurs de Chine. Ce dense réseau de palais, portes monumentales et cours était à la fois résidence impériale et capitale administrative, et ce malgré les assauts périodiques des termites et des typhons. En 1945, lorsque Bao Dai, le dernier empereur, abdique, la Cité interdite s'enorgueillit de douzaines de pavillons et de centaines de pièces. Toutes ses merveilles ont volé en éclat en 1968 sous les bombardements de l'armée américaine, en représailles à la prise de Hué par les communistes. Des rizières recouvrent maintenant une grande partie du site de l'ancienne résidence royale. Les quelques rares bâtiments conservés montrent comment les Vietnamiens interprétaient l'architecture impériale chinoise.

❋ **PREVIOUS PAGES** Built in 1833, the Noon Gate could only be used by the emperor. The palace of Supreme Harmony housed the throne of the Nguyen dynasty. Plasterwork: image of the five-nailed dragon, symbol of imperial power. **ABOVE** Le van Luong, a mandarin, attired in court dress. ❋ **VORHERGEHENDE DOPPELSEITEN** Das Mittagstor aus dem Jahr 1833 wurde einzig und allein vom Kaiser benutzt. In der Halle der höchsten Harmonie stand der Thron der Nguyen-Dynastie. Stuckarbeiten: Drachen mit fünf Nägeln, einem Symbol der kaiserlichen Macht. **OBEN** Le Van Luong, ein Mandarin, in der Kleidung des Hofes. ❋ **DOUBLE PAGES PRECEDENTES** Construite en 1833, la porte du Midi était réservée à l'empereur. Le palais de la Suprême Harmonie abritait le trône de la dynastie Nguyên. Décoration en plâtre: le dragon à cinq griffes, symbole du pouvoir impérial. **CI-DESSUS** le Van Luong, haut fonctionnaire en habit de cour.

A FORMER MANDARIN'S HOME

HUÉ

An imperial retainer takes his last bow.

For nearly 150 years the Nguyen dynasty ruled from the Forbidden Purple City.

The royal complex housed a vast number of hereditary mandarins whose life was inextricably linked to the ruler. Le Van Luong, seen with his wife on the facing page, was among them; like his father, he was a military mandarin. Le Van Luong was born in 1920, a few years before Bao Dai, the last emperor of Vietnam, ascended the throne. He was in royal service from 1940 to 1954. It was a tumultuous time. In 1945 the French-educated Bao Dai went into exile when Ho Chi Minh's Communist guerillas expelled the occupying Japanese. Four years later the French, in an attempt to legitimize their regime, put Bao Dai back on the throne. But the "Playboy Emperor" proved a feeble puppet. He went back to France in 1955 and died there in 1997. It was the end of an era. Le Van Luong has lived at the cusp of sudden and dramatic changes. He now occupies a small house, originally made of wood, that his father built. About 20 years ago it was renovated in concrete. For him that is the final change.

Die Nguyen-Dynastie herrschte fast 150 Jahre von der Verbotenen Purpurnen Stadt aus.

In der kaiserlichen Palastanlage wohnten zahlreiche Mandarine, deren Amt jeweils ererbt und deren Leben unwiderruflich mit dem des Herrschers verbunden war. Wie sein Vater war auch Le Van Luong einer von ihnen, ein Militärmandarin (links, mit seiner Frau). Le Van Luong ist 1920 geboren – nur wenige Jahre, bevor der letzte Kaiser von Vietnam, Bao Dai, den Thron bestieg. In den ereignisreichen Jahren von 1940 bis 1954 diente er dem Kaiser. Als die kommunistische Guerilla Ho Chi Minhs 1945 die Besetzung des Landes durch die Japaner beendete, ging Bao Dai ins französische Exil. Vier Jahre später setzten die Franzosen ihn in dem Versuch, ihr Regime zu legitimieren, wieder auf den Thron. Der »Playboy-Kaiser« entpuppte sich jedoch als willenlose Marionette und kehrte 1955 nach Frankreich zurück, wo er 1997 starb. Das war das Ende einer Ära. Le Van Luong, der die dramatischen Veränderungen in seinem Land hautnah miterlebte, wohnt inzwischen in einem kleinen Haus, das sein Vater ursprünglich aus Holz erbaut hat. Vor zwanzig Jahren ließ er es in Beton überholen – aus seiner Sicht die letzte Veränderung.

Pendant près de 150 ans, la dynastie des Nguyên a régné depuis la Cité pourpre interdite.

La résidence royale abritait alors un très grand nombre de mandarins héréditaires dont la vie était indissociable de celle du souverain. Le Van Luong, que l'on voit ici avec sa femme, en faisait partie. Tout comme son père, c'était un mandarin d'épée. Le Van Luong est né en 1920, quelques années avant que Bao Dai, le dernier empereur du Viêt-nam, ne monte sur le trône. Il a été au service du souverain de 1940 à 1954, une période agitée dans l'histoire du pays : en 1945, Bao Dai, qui avait reçu une éducation française, a pris le chemin de l'exil lorsque les rebelles communistes d'Ho Chi Minh ont bouté l'occupant japonais hors du pays. Quatre ans plus tard, les Français, soucieux de légitimer leur régime, ont remis Bao Dai sur le trône. Mais cet empereur «playboy» n'était qu'un fantoche. En 1955, il est retourné en France, où il est décédé en 1997. La fin d'une ère avait sonné. Le Van Luong, qui a vécu en première ligne ces changements spectaculaires, vit maintenant dans une maison modeste, construite par son père. Il y a une vingtaine d'années, il a utilisé du béton pour rénover cette maison qui était à l'origine en bois. Pour lui, les transformations s'arrêtent là.

※ **LEFT** a small altar dedicated to ancestor worship. **BELOW** the main shrine to the Buddha on an old carved cabinet. **FACING PAGE** Le Van Luong's living quarters. ※ **LINKS** ein kleiner Altar zur Verehrung der Vorfahren. **UNTEN** der Hauptschrein für Buddha auf einem alten holzgeschnitzten Schrank. **RECHTE SEITE** Le Van Luongs Wohnbereich. ※ **A GAUCHE** Cet autel de dimensions réduites sert au culte des ancêtres. **CI-DESSOUS** L'autel du Bouddha a été aménagé sur un meuble ancien en bois sculpté. **PAGE DE DROITE** les appartements de Le Van Luong.

THE TEMPLE OF PRINCESS NGOC SON

HUÉ

Feng Shui breathes in a royal past.

Phan Thuan An modestly describes himself as a researcher of the history, culture and architecture of his city but he is, in fact, a scholar steeped in its remarkable heritage.

Hué has always been a centre of artistic, religious and scholarly pursuits in Vietnam. For nearly 150 years it was also a political capital. Its royal past is commemorated in an impressive citadel, splendid tombs and pagodas. Phan Thuan An's garden house was built in 1921 by Prince Nguyen Huu Tien, consort of Princess Ngoc Son, second daughter of Emperor Dong Khanh who ruled the country in the late 19th century. The house was planned strictly along Feng Shui principles, with elements such as the screen, the pond, the dragon and the tiger placed in front. Born in a village outside the city, Phan Thuan An married a granddaughter of the man who built the house and so became its custodian. Since inheriting the home in 1965, he has strived to preserve its original character as part of conserving a gift from his ancestors: "for my family, my city and for everybody".

Phan Thuan An bezeichnet sich bescheiden als Forscher in der Geschichte, Kultur und Architektur seiner Stadt; doch er ist ein Gelehrter, der von dem bemerkenswerten Erbe Huês durchdrungen ist.

Huê war von jeher ein künstlerisches wie religiöses Zentrum der Gelehrsamkeit und auch über hundertfünfzig Jahre die Hauptstadt des Landes. Die Erinnerung an die kaiserliche Vergangenheit wird in der großartigen Zitadelle, den wundervollen Gräbern und Pagoden bewahrt. Prinz Nguyen Huu Tien ließ 1921 Phan Thuan Ans Gartenhaus erbauen. Er war der Gatte der Prinzessin Ngoc Son, der zweiten Tochter des Kaisers Dong Khanh, der im späten 19. Jahrhundert über das Land herrschte. Das Haus wurde streng nach den Prinzipien des Feng Shui entworfen, die beispielsweise die Trennwand, den Teich, den Drachen und den Tiger am Eingang vorsehen. Phan Thuan An, der aus einem Dorf in der Nähe Huês stammt, heiratete eine Enkelin des Mannes, der das Haus erbaut hatte, und wurde so zu seinem Hüter. Seit er es 1965 erbte, hat er sich stets bemüht, seinen ursprünglichen Charakter im Sinne eines Geschenkes seiner Vorfahren zu bewahren: »für meine Familie, meine Stadt und für alle Anderen.«

Phan Thuan An se définit, avec beaucoup de modestie, comme un chercheur de l'histoire, de la culture et de l'architecture de sa ville, mais c'est en fait un érudit imprégné de son patrimoine historique.

Hué a toujours été un centre artistique, religieux et intellectuel majeur du Viêt-nam, dont il a aussi été la capitale politique pendant 150 ans. Une citadelle impressionnante, des mausolées magnifiques et des pagodes témoignent de son passé royal. Le pavillon de jardin dans lequel Phan Thuan An vit actuellement a été construit en 1921, par le prince Nguyên Huu Tien. Ce dernier avait épousé la princesse Ngoc Son, fille cadette de l'empereur Dong Khanh qui a régné sur le pays à la fin du 19e siècle. La maison a été construite selon les principes du Feng Shui : elle intègre des éléments tels que l'écran, le bassin, et l'association du dragon et du tigre devant la maison. En épousant la petite-fille de l'homme qui a construit la maison, Phan Thuan An, originaire d'un village à quelque distance de Hué, en est devenu le gardien. Depuis qu'il en a hérité en 1965, il s'est toujours efforcé d'en préserver le caractère d'origine, comme l'on conserve précieusement un bien que l'on tient d'un ancêtre, «pour ma famille, ma ville et pour tous ».

✳ **PREVIOUS PAGE, ABOVE FACING AND FOLLOWING PAGES** Phan Thuan An at work in his study. The table with dragon-shaped legs is inlaid with copper and mother-of-pearl. The central space is occupied by the family's Buddhist temple. ✳ **VORHERGEHENDE, DIESE UND FOLGENDE DOPPELSEITEN** Phan Thuan An bei der Arbeit in seinem Studio. Der Tisch hat drachenförmige Beine. Das Zentrum des Hauses nimmt der familieneigene Buddha-Tempel ein. ✳ **PAGES PRECEDENTES, CETTES-CI ET SUIVANTES** Phan Thuan An dans son bureau. La table ronde reposant sur des pieds en forme de dragon est incrustée de cuivre et de nacre. Au cœur de la maison, l'autel bouddhique de la famille.

GARDEN HOUSE ON THE PERFUME RIVER

HUÉ

Peace and poetry by the Perfume River.

Xuan Hoa village is a short distance from the centre of Hué. Here, on the banks of the Perfume River, is one of the last remaining houses of old Indochina.

Appropriately called the "Peaceful Mansion" it was built in 1895 for a daughter of the Emperor Duc Duc, fifth of the 13 Nguyen monarchs. Its chequered history included ownership by a high-ranking mandarin's family and a provincial governor. The house also mirrors the shifts of power in north Vietnam, from feudal to French colonial times followed by the Communist takeover under Ho Chi Minh. The governor's widow Dao Thi Xuan Yen, who lived here, was by all accounts extraordinary. A school principal and nationalist, she maintained a fine balance in the changing political order and died childless in 1997. Nguyen Dinh Chau is her grand nephew. He worked in Saigon as an accountant for a French firm but returned home after the war. His wife and children live in Paris. Nguyen Dinh Chau's passion is literature. He spends his days reading and composing poetry in the house on the Perfume River.

Im Dorf Xuan Hoa – unweit des Zentrums von Huê, am Ufer des Parfümflusses – liegt eines der letzten erhaltenen Häuser des alten Indochina.

Die »Villa der Ruhe«, wie sie zu Recht genannt wird, wurde 1895 für eine Tochter des Kaisers Duc Duc, dem fünften der 13 Nguyen-Monarchen erbaut. In ihrer bewegten Vergangenheit gehörte die Villa unter anderem der Familie eines hochrangigen Mandarins und einem Provinzgouverneur. Sie spiegelt auch die Machtverschiebungen in Nordvietnam vom Feudalismus über die französische Kolonialherrschaft bis zu der Eroberung durch die Kommunisten unter Ho Chi Minh wider. Die Witwe des Gouverneurs, Dao Thi Xuan Yen, lebte ebenfalls in diesem Haus; sie war den Berichten nach eine außergewöhnliche Persönlichkeit. Als kinderlose Schulrektorin und Nationalistin wusste sie sich bis zu ihrem Tod 1997 zu behaupten, wechselnder politischer Machtverhältnisse zum Trotz. Ihr Großneffe Nguyen Dinh Chau arbeitete für ein französisches Unternehmen in Saigon, kehrte jedoch nach dem Krieg nach Hause zurück. Seine Frau und seine Kinder leben in Paris. Da Nguyen Dinh Chau sich sehr für Literatur interessiert, verbringt er seine Tage damit, in seinem Haus am Parfümfluss Gedichte zu lesen und zu schreiben.

C'est dans le village de Xuan Hoa, à deux pas du centre de Hué, que s'élève sur les berges de la rivière aux Parfums l'une des dernières maisons de l'ancienne Indochine.

Appelée fort à propos la «demeure paisible», elle a été construite en 1895 par une fille de l'empereur Duc Duc, le cinquième des 13 monarques de la dynastie Nguyên. Dans son histoire à rebondissements, elle a eu comme propriétaires une famille de très hauts fonctionnaires et un gouverneur de province et elle a été le témoin des changements de pouvoir au Viêtnam du Nord, du système féodal à l'ère coloniale française, puis de l'instauration d'une république démocratique que sous la présidence de Ho Chi Minh. La veuve du gouverneur Dao Thi Xuan Yen, qui vivait dans cette maison, était une femme extraordinaire. Directrice d'école et nationaliste, elle a maintenu son cap dans les bouleversements politiques et est morte en 1997, sans laisser de descendance. C'est son petit-neveu Nguyên Dinh Chau qui en a hérité. Il a travaillé à Saigon comme comptable dans une entreprise française avant de rentrer chez lui après la guerre. Sa femme et ses enfants vivent à Paris. Passionné de littérature, il passe ses journées à lire et composer des poèmes dans sa maison sur les rives de la rivière aux parfums.

※ **BELOW** At the centre of the house is the family shrine with an image of the Buddha. **FACING PAGE** The dining room, like the rest of the house, is built of ironwood panels. ※ **UNTEN** In der Mitte des Hauses steht der Familienschrein mit einer Buddhafigur. **RECHTE SEITE** Wie die anderen Räume wurde auch das Esszimmer mit einer Eisenholztäfelung verkleidet. ※ **CI-DESSOUS** L'autel familial avec son bouddha se trouve au cœur de la maison. **PAGE DE DROITE** Comme les autres pièces de la maison, la salle à manger est lambrissée de bois de fer.

※ **FACING PAGE** Most surfaces in Nguyen Dinh Chau's bedroom are covered with books and papers. **ABOVE** The 76-year-old scholar and poet spends his days reading and composing poetry. ※ **LINKE SEITE** In Nguyen Dinh Chaus Schlafzimmer stapeln sich Bücher und Dokumente, wo immer sie sich ablegen lassen. **OBEN** Der 76-jährige Gelehrte und Dichter verbringt seine Tage mit dem Lesen und Verfassen von Gedichten. ※ **PAGE DE GAUCHE** La chambre de Nguyên Dinh Chau est investie par les livres et les papiers. **CI-DESSUS** Cet érudit et poète de 76 ans consacre le plus clair de son temps à la lecture et à la poésie.

※ **ABOVE AND FACING PAGE** Separate men's and women's quarters flank the family shrine in the centre. The Chinese incense burner and crystal vases are heirlooms. The supporting columns are made of jackfruit wood. ※ **OBEN UND RECHTE SEITE** Von dem Familienschrein in der Mitte gehen rechts und links die getrennten Gemächer der Frauen und Männer ab. Der chinesische Räucherkerzenhalter und die Kristallvasen sind Erbstücke. Die stützenden Säulen sind aus Jackfruchtholz. ※ **CI-DESSUS ET PAGE DE DROITE** les appartements des femmes étant séparés de ceux des hommes par l'autel familial. Le brûle-encens et les vases en cristal sont des héritages. Les colonnes soutenant le plafond sont en bois de jaquier.

THE Hoi An Bridge

Hoi An

In the lingering shadows of old Japan.

No one is quite sure when Hoi An Bridge, also known as the Pagoda Bridge, was built but it's likely that Japanese merchants commissioned it during the era of the Edo shoguns in the early 17th century.

Under Vietnam's Nguyen overlords the Japanese were a large community in Hoi An, permitted to build freely. The idea behind the bridge was to link the Japanese quarter of town with the Chinese quarter across a small stream. In fact, its name in Vietnamese, *Lai Vien Kieu*, translates as "Bridge for Passers-by from Afar". Unlike Vietnamese or Chinese decoration which can be florid, the bridge is chaste in design, with roof tiles capped by blue and white porcelain bowls. It was covered to protect pedestrians from sun and rain. Built into the Hoi An Bridge is a small temple; inscriptions behind the seated temple scholar, on the facing page, list the donors who contributed to a restoration. The bridge entrances are guarded by monkey and dog sculptures, in memory of Japan's emperors, many of whom were born in the years of the monkey and dog, respectively.

Das Baujahr der Hoi-An-Brücke ist unbekannt, wahrscheinlich aber wurde die Pagodenbrücke von japanischen Kaufleuten in der Zeit der Edo-Shogune im frühen 17. Jahrhundert in Auftrag gegeben.

Während die Nguyen über Vietnam herrschten, gab es eine große japanische Gemeinde in Hoi An, deren Mitglieder ungehindert bauen durften. Die Brücke über einen kleinen Fluss sollte das japanische und das chinesische Viertel miteinander verbinden. Der vietnamesische Name der Brücke, *Lai Vien Kieu*, bedeutet »Brücke für Passanten aus der Ferne«. Im Gegensatz zu den eher blumigen vietnamesischen oder chinesischen Dekorationsstilen wirkt die Brücke, deren Dachziegel mit blauweißen Schalen verziert sind, eher schlicht. Sie wurde überdacht, um die Passanten vor Regen und Sonne zu schützen. Auch einen kleinen Tempel gibt es auf der Hoi-An-Brücke. Die Inschriften hinter dem sitzenden Tempelgelehrten (Bild links) bezeichnen die Sponsoren, die zur Restauration beigetragen haben. Die Eingänge zur Brücke werden von Affen- und Hundeskulpturen bewacht – dies als Erinnerung an jene japanischen Kaiser, die im Jahr des Affen oder des Hundes geboren sind.

Personne ne sait au juste quand le pont de Hoi An, aussi appelé le «pont japonais», a été construit, mais il est probable que des commerçants japonais ont commandé sa construction pendant l'ère Edo, au début du 17e siècle.

Sous la dynastie de Nguyên, les Japonais représentaient une communauté importante à Hoi An et avaient le droit de construire sans autorisation préalable. Ce pont était censé relier le quartier japonais de la ville au quartier chinois situé de l'autre côté d'un petit cours d'eau, d'où son nom vietnamien de *Lai Vien Kieu*, «pont pour les voyageurs venus de loin». Contrairement aux constructions de styles vietnamien et chinois qui peuvent être très richement ornementées, ce pont est décoré très sobrement: seules des coupelles en porcelaine bleue et blanche agrémentent la toiture dont il a été doté pour protéger les piétons des intempéries. Le pont abrite un petit temple; derrière l'érudit du temple (photo page de gauche), on peut voir la liste des donateurs ayant contribué à sa restauration. L'entrée du pont est gardée par des singes et des chiens sculptés, en souvenir des empereurs japonais, nés pour la plupart au cours de l'année du singe ou du chien.

Tran Quoc Pagoda

Hanoi

A Buddhist landmark in the city of the Soaring Dragon.

Despite its modern development, the Vietnamese capital retains much of the leisurely style and period elegance of a refined old city.

The words *Ha Noi* mean "City in the Bend of the River". In an earlier age Hanoi was called "The City of the Soaring Dragon". Both the Red River and a number of lakes, public parks, old markets and yellow-painted French colonial villas give it a special charm. Scattered throughout are a number of monuments. The Tran Quoc Pagoda, nestled between the West Lake and the Truc Bach Lake, is among the most ancient of Buddhist temples in Hanoi. It was founded in the 6th century but was moved to its present location in the early 17th century. Besides a pantheon of Buddha statues, it houses an impressive collection of stupas. In Tran Quoc's tranquil gardens stands a bodhi tree, taken from a cutting of the original tree under which the Buddha attained enlightenment.

Die Hauptstadt Vietnams bewahrt trotz moderner Entwicklung viel von dem gemächlichen Tempo und der zeitlosen Eleganz einer vornehmen alten Stadt.

Ha Noi bedeutet »Stadt in der Flusskurve«. In einem früheren Zeitalter wurde Hanoi »Stadt des aufsteigenden Drachens« genannt. Ihren besonderen Charme verdankt die Stadt neben dem Roten Fluss mehreren Seen, öffentlichen Parkanlagen, alten Märkten und den gelb getünchten französischen Villen. Zahlreiche Denkmäler zieren die geschichtsträchtige Stadt. Die Tran-Quoc-Pagode, die sich zwischen den Westsee und den Truc-Bach-See schmiegt, zählt zu den ältesten buddhistischen Tempeln Hanois. Sie wurde im 6. Jahrhundert erbaut, aber erst im frühen 17. Jahrhundert an ihren heutigen Ort verlegt. Neben einem Pantheon von Buddhastatuen beherbergt die Pagode eine beeindruckende Stupa-Sammlung. In dem stillen Garten Tran Quocs steht ein Bodhi-Baum, der aus einem Ableger des Baumes spross, unter dem Buddha die Erleuchtung widerfuhr.

Malgré son occidentalisation, la capitale vietnamienne est encore empreinte de la légèreté et de l'élégance d'une ville au glorieux passé.

Ha Noi signifie «Province entourée de rivières». A une époque plus ancienne, Hanoi s'appelait la «Cité du dragon prenant son envol». Cette ville doit son charme particulier au fleuve Rouge, à une profusion de lacs, de jardins publics, de vieux marchés et de villas coloniales françaises peintes en jaune et aux nombreux monuments disséminés dans la ville. La pagode de Tran Quoc, lovée entre le lac de l'Ouest et le lac Truc Bach, est l'un des temples bouddhiques les plus anciens de Hanoi. Construite au 6e siècle, elle a été transférée au début du 17e siècle à l'emplacement qu'elle occupe actuellement. Outre un panthéon de statues de Bouddha, elle s'enorgueillit d'une impressionnante collection de stupas. En se promenant dans les jardins paisibles de Tran Quoc, on tombe sur un arbre bodhi, un rejeton de celui sous lequel le Bouddha est parvenu à l'éveil.

※ **PREVIOUS PAGES** the courtyard of the main temple. funerary stupas around the pagoda. Buddha images in the temple's gilded altar. **ABOVE** The stone tablet reads the history of the pagoda. ※ **VORHERGEHENDE DOPPELSEITEN** der Hof des Haupttempels. Bestattungs-*Stupas* um die Pagode. Buddhafiguren auf dem vergoldeten Altar des Tempels. **OBEN** Die Geschichte der Pagode ist in einer Steintafel eingraviert. ※ **DOUBLES PAGES PRECEDENTES** la cour du temple principal. Des stupas abritant des reliques encerclent la pagode. Des bouddhas sont exposés sur l'autel doré du temple. **CI-DESSUS** l'histoire de la pagode est gravée sur une tablette en pierre.

Sandra and Yan d'Auriol

The China Club

Hong Kong

THE CHINA CLUB
HONG KONG

All the vogue is retro-Chinese style.

David Tang was an academic in Hong Kong until the age of thirty, when he realized that he wanted to go into business.

The utilitarian and often standardized look of hotels, shopping malls, restaurant and club interiors puzzled him. Why was there so little room for pictures or sculpture? Other than art, why was there no drama, a sense of pure theatre in places where people met to enjoy a meal or a drink? The China Club, atop the grand old Bank of China building in central Hong Kong, was his first business venture. Tang aimed to evoke an atmosphere of Shanghai in the Thirties. His imagination was backed by a relentless search for the right art and fittings: Chinoiserie lamps bought in Paris and Budapest, sofas acquired at auction and in London clubs, artworks from Communist China or commissioned from Chinese artists. Nothing has changed in Hong Kong's China Club since it opened twelve years ago. But David Tang's idea has flowered to include branches in Beijing and Singapore.

Bis zu seinem dreißigsten Geburtstag lehrte David Tang an einer Universität in Hongkong. Doch dann beschloss er, Geschäftsmann zu werden.

Wie viele Hotels, Einkaufspassagen, Restaurants und Clubs in einem gleichen, einheitlichen Stil eingerichtet waren, hatte ihn seit langem irritiert. Warum wurde Bildern und Skulpturen so wenig Raum gegeben? Abgesehen von Bildender Kunst fragte er sich, warum nicht auch theatralische Elemente die Räume mit gestalten sollten, in denen Menschen gesellig zu Speis und Trank zusammen kommen. Als Erstes eröffnete Tang den China Club in Hongkong – mitten in der Stadt, ganz oben im alten Gebäude der Bank of China. Die Clubatmosphäre beschwört das Shanghai der 1930er Jahre herauf, nicht zuletzt, weil Tang sich weltweit die passenden Kunstwerke und Einrichtungsgegenstände besorgte. In Paris und Budapest kaufte er Chinoiserie-Lampen, während er Sofas auf Auktionen und in Londoner Clubs ersteigerte. Viele Kunstwerke fand er im kommunistischen China oder wurden bei zeitgenössischen Künstlern in Auftrag gegeben. Seit der Eröffnung vor zwölf Jahren hat David Tang im China Club Hongkong nichts verändert, aber inzwischen entstanden weitere Filialen in Peking und Singapur.

David Tang faisait carrière à l'université de Hong-Kong, et puis, à trente ans, il a décidé de se lancer dans les affaires.

Il s'était souvent interrogé sur l'aspect utilitaire et souvent standardisé des hôtels, des centres commerciaux, des restaurants et des intérieurs de clubs: pourquoi y faisait-on si peu de place aux arts picturaux et à la sculpture? Et puis, abstraction faite de l'art, pourquoi ne trouve-t-on aucune théâtralité dans les endroits où les gens se retrouvent autour d'un repas ou d'un verre? C'est ainsi que David Tang s'est lancé dans sa première aventure commerciale, le China Club, juché au faîte de la Bank of China, au cœur de Hong-Kong. Son objectif était de récréer l'atmosphère du Shanghai des années 1930. Ce qu'il a fait en cherchant les objets d'art ou utilitaires appropriés: des lampes – chinoiseries trouvées à Paris et Budapest –, des sofas achetés dans des ventes aux enchères ou dans des clubs londoniens, et des œuvres d'art provenant de la Chine communiste ou commandées à des artistes chinois. Rien n'a changé dans le China Club de Hong-Kong depuis son ouverture au début des années 1990, mais le concept a fait florès: Pékin et Singapour ont maintenant aussi leur China Club.

长征吧 THE LONG MARCH BAR

※ **PREVIOUS PAGES, CLOCKWISE FROM TOP LEFT** The theme of the "Long March Bar" commemorates the Communist Party's success. An old telephone under a chinoiserie lamp bought in Paris. The tinted glass door panels were designed by David Tang. **FACING PAGE** a corner of the dining room. **ABOVE** The fan-shaped panel high on the dining room wall advertises special teas. ※
VORHERGEHENDE DOPPELSEITEN, IM UHRZEIGERSINN VON LINKS OBEN Das Motiv der »Bar des Langen Marsches« erinnert an den Erfolg der Kommunistischen Partei. Ein altes Telefon unter einer Chinoiserie-Lampe aus Paris. Die bunten Glastüren wurden von David Tang entworfen. **LINKE SEITE** Blick in den Speisesaal. **OBEN** Die fächerförmige Wandtafel im Speisesaal (über der Glastür links) wirbt für ausgewählte Teesorten. ※ **DOUBLE PAGE PRECEDENTE, DANS LE SENS DES AIGUILLES D'UNE MONTRE, À PARTIR D'EN HAUT À GAUCHE** Le « Bar de la Longue Marche » célèbre la victoire du parti communiste. Le téléphone ancien sous une lampe a été acheté à Paris. Les portes vitrées teintées sont signées David Tang. **PAGE DE GAUCHE** quelques tables de la salle à manger. **CI-DESSUS** Le panneau en forme d'éventail sur le mur du fond est une carte des thés spéciaux.

Sandra and Yan D'Auriol
Hong Kong

Open to the breezes.

Hong Kong is hilly and slopes steeply down to swathes of water on all sides. One of the best views is from Repulse Bay to the south of the island.

Built into a hillside, Sandra and Yan d'Auriol found one of the few remaining post-war houses divided into duplex apartments. High ceilings, wooden floors and generous spaces harked to a bygone era. Sandra is English, a jewellery designer whose family has been in Asia for four generations. Over the years she has developed an obsession for Chinese pots, some 4000 years old yet completely modern in form. Yan is French, runs a trading business, and likes simple, oversize objects. For more than two decades they have collected Asian antiques. They worked together in decorating the family home with the principal objective of exercising restraint. "White walls, dark floors and we let the objects do the rest," says Sandra. Rare in Hong Kong is the terrace which rings with birdsong in the morning and where they often entertain in the evenings.

Hongkong ist hügelig und fällt allseits steil zum Wasser ab. Von der Repulse Bay eröffnet sich ein großartiger Ausblick auf den Süden der Insel.

Sandra und Yan d'Auriol hatten das Glück, eines der wenigen erhaltenen, in den Hügel gebauten Nachkriegshäuser mit zweistöckigen Wohnungen zu finden. Die hohen Decken, Holzböden und geräumigen Zimmer verweisen auf längst vergangene Zeiten. Die Engländerin Sandra, deren Familie seit vier Generationen in Asien ansässig ist, entwirft Schmuck. Mit den Jahren entwickelte sie eine Sammelleidenschaft für chinesische Gefäße, die zum Teil 4000 Jahre alt sind, zugleich aber höchst modern in der Form. Der Franzose Yan leitet ein Handelsunternehmen und hat eine Vorliebe für schlichte Dinge in Übergröße. Die beiden sammeln seit mehr als zwanzig Jahren asiatische Antiquitäten und nahmen sich bei der Einrichtung vor, möglichst viel Zurückhaltung zu üben. »Weiße Wände, dunkle Böden, den Rest überlassen wir den Objekten«, sagt Sandra. Die Terrasse, auf der morgens die Vögel singen und das Ehepaar abends häufig Gäste empfängt, ist in Hongkong etwas Besonderes.

Hong-Kong est escarpée, ses collines descendent à pic dans les flots tumultueux qui l'entourent. De Repulse Bay a la plus belle vue sur le sud de l'île.

Sandra et Yan d'Auriol ont trouvé, accrochée à flanc de coteau, l'une des dernières maisons en duplex de l'après-guerre. Plafonds hauts, parquets et espaces généreux évoquaient des temps révolus. Sandra est issue d'une famille anglaise établie en Asie depuis quatre générations. Cette créatrice de bijoux s'est prise de passion au fil des ans pour les poteries chinoises, dont certaines pièces de sa collection, vieilles de plus de 4000 ans, ont une forme très moderne. Yan est français, fait du négoce et aime les objets simples surdimensionnés. Depuis plus de vingt ans, ils collectionnent les antiquités asiatiques. C'est ensemble qu'ils ont conçu la décoration de leur maison, avec comme maître mot, la sobriété. « Des murs blancs et des sols sombres, et nous laissons aux objets le soin de faire le reste », explique Sandra. Ils possèdent une rareté à Hong-Kong : une terrasse qui retentit du chant des oiseaux à l'aube et sur laquelle ils reçoivent souvent le soir.

FACING PAGE A wooden Chinese screen behind the opium bed and a lacquer box are reflected in an antique inscribed mirror in the bedroom. ABOVE A Han dynasty dog sculpture and Sung dynasty pots displayed on a Chinese altar table. BELOW A primitive Indonesian sculpture and touches of silk in Peking yellow enliven the sitting room. ❈ LINKE SEITE In einem antiken Spiegel mit eingravierten Schriftzeichen spiegeln sich im Vordergrund eine Lacktruhe sowie eine chinesische Trennwand aus Holz hinter dem Opiumbett. OBEN eine Hundeskulptur aus der Han-Epoche und Gefäße aus der Sung-Zeit auf einem chinesischen Altartisch. UNTEN Eine primitive indonesische Skulptur und Akzente in pekinggelber Seide beleben das Wohnzimmer. ❈ PAGE DE GAUCHE Dans la chambre, un miroir ancien gravé reflète le paravent chinois en bois derrière le lit à opium et la boîte en laque. CI-DESSUS Une sculpture han représentant un chien et des récipients song sont disposés sur une table-autel chinoise. CI-DESSOUS Une sculpture primitive indonésienne et les accents de la soie jaune impérial agrémentent le salon.

The Funiture House

Leonardo Griglie

Jehanne de Biolley and
Harrison Liu

Pascale
Desvaux

The Bamboo Wall

Pia Pierre

The Forbidden City

The Grand Hyatt

Fuchun Resort

The China Club

e Red Capital Residence

CHina

THE BAMBOO WALL

BEiJing

Zen purity in the shadow of the Great Wall.

The Great Wall of China was not a singular enterprise. It was built in sections by different dynasties over centuries, partly as a fortification and partly as a highway for men and materials.

Some of it dates back to 2000 years ago; large parts have crumbled or been restored. Snaking across rugged terrain to the Gobi Desert, it is an awesome symbol of history, legend and the modern tourist industry. One popular location to view it is at Badaling, 70 kilometres. northwest of Beijing; it is here that developers Zhang Xin and her husband Pan Shiyi, in a bold personal initiative, hit upon the idea of inviting 12 leading Asian architects to design villas in a self-styled commune. The models of avant-garde architecture were exhibited at the Venice Biennale in 2002 and acquired by the Centre Pompidou in Paris. Inspired by the seamless integration of the Great Wall in a rough landscape and the use of bamboo as scaffolding, Japanese architect Kengo Kuma sought a harmony between "delicacy and roughness". In tribute he calls the house the "Bamboo Wall".

Die Große Mauer war nicht das Projekt eines Einzelnen, sondern wurde über Jahrhunderte in Teilabschnitten unter mehreren Dynastien errichtet. Sie diente der Verteidigung, aber auch dem Transport von Menschen und Waren.

Einige Abschnitte der Großen Mauer sind 2000 Jahre alt, andernorts ist sie zerbröckelt oder neu aufgebaut worden. Als wundersames legendenreiches Symbol der chinesischen Geschichte und Ziel zahlreicher Touristen aus aller Herren Länder windet sie sich durch die zerklüftete Landschaft bis zur Wüste Gobi. 70 Kilometer nordwestlich von Peking liegt Badaling, ein beliebter Ausflugsort für einen Besuch der Großen Mauer. Hier kamen die Immobilienmaklerin Zhang Xin und ihr Mann Pan Shiyi auf die Idee, zwölf führende asiatische Architekten zur Gestaltung von Villen in einer eigens gestalteten Kommune einzuladen. Die Modelle dieser avantgardistischen Architektur wurden 2002 auf der Biennale in Venedig ausgestellt und vom Centre Pompidou in Paris erworben. Der japanische Architekt Kengo Kuma ließ sich davon inspirieren, wie nahtlos die Mauer sich in die raue Landschaft einfügt, und auf Basis eines Gerüsts aus Bambus suchte er eine harmonischen Verbindung von »Feinheit und Härte«. Entsprechend gab er dem Haus den Namen »Bamboo Wall«.

La Grande Muraille de Chine n'a pas été l'œuvre d'un souverain, mais de différentes dynasties qui l'ont construite par étapes au fil des siècles. C'était à la fois une fortification et un axe de communication.

Certains de ses tronçons sont vieux de 2000 ans, d'autres ont été restaurés ou sont totalement tombés en ruine. Serpentant sur un terrain accidenté jusqu'au désert de Gobi, la Grande Muraille est chargée d'histoire et de légende. Pour découvrir ce site touristique majeur, il est recommandé de se rendre à Badaling, à 70 km au nord-ouest de Pékin. C'est là que Zhang Xin et Pan Shiyi, un couple de promoteurs immobiliers n'ayant pas froid aux yeux, ont eu l'idée d'inviter 12 grands architectes asiatiques à concevoir des villas dans une résidence. Les maquettes de cette architecture avant-gardiste ont été exposées à la biennale de Venise en 2002, puis acquises par le Centre Georges Pompidou. Inspiré par la parfaite intégration de la Grande Muraille dans un paysage inhospitalier et l'utilisation du bambou comme élément de construction d'échafaudages, l'architecte japonais Kengo Kuma a recherché un équilibre entre «délicatesse et rudesse». Tout naturellement la maison s'est appelée le «Bamboo Wall» (Muraille de Bambou).

ABOVE AND FACING PAGE Kengo Kuma's "Bamboo Wall" house sits on rugged, untamed slopes like the Great Wall itself. **BOTTOM** Rough stone steps lead to the main entrance. ✳ **OBEN UND RECHTE SEITE OBEN** Kengo Kumas Haus »Bamboo Wall« steht wie die Große Mauer inmitten zerklüfteter wilder Böschungen. **RECHTE SEITE UNTEN** Eine Treppe aus grobem Stein führt zum Haupteingang. ✳ **CI-DESSUS ET PAGE DE DROITE, EN HAUT** Comme la Grande Muraille, la maison conçue par Kengo Kuma est située dans un environnement accidenté et sauvage. **EN BAS** Un escalier de pierres brutes mène à l'entrée principale.

※ **FACING PAGE** The living room's plate glass wall overlooks the wild landscape of the hills around the Great Wall. Moveable bamboo walls line the façade of the house. **ABOVE** A bamboo pavilion, surrounded by a water body, is used as a tea house for contemplation. ※ **LINKE SEITE** Ausblick durch die Panoramafenster auf die raue Landschaft in den Hügeln unweit der Großen Mauer. Schiebewände aus Bambus verkleiden die Fassade. **OBEN** In dem von Wasser umgebenen Pavillon aus Bambus wird zur Entspannung Tee serviert. ※ **PAGE DE GAUCHE** La baie vitrée du salon découvre le paysage sauvage de collines aux abords de la Grande Muraille. Des parois amovibles en bambou habillent la façade de la maison. **CI-DESSUS** Ce pavillon de thé en bambou entouré d'eau invite à la contemplation.

FACING PAGE Kengo Kuma used bamboo of varying degrees of density, delicacy and roughness to achieve the graded textures of the tea pavilion. **ABOVE** Plate glass walls in the dining room integrate the use of bamboo indoors and outdoors. ❋ **LINKE SEITE** Kengo Kuma verwendete unterschiedlich dichten, feinen und rauen Bambus für die abgestufte Struktur des Teepavillons. **OBEN** Die Panoramafenster im Esszimmer integrieren den innen und außen verwendeten Bambus. ❋ **PAGE DE GAUCHE** Kengo Kuma a utilisé des bambous plus ou moins épais et présentant des surfaces lisses ou rugueuses pour obtenir le dégradé de textures du pavillon de thé. **CI-DESSUS** Les parois vitrées révèlent la double utilisation du bambou à l'intérieur et à l'extérieur.

THE FURNITURE HOUSE BEIJING

A serendipitous discovery of bamboo.

A couple of surprises awaited Japanese architect Shigeru Ban when he was among the twelve Asian architects invited to design villas as part of an experimental hotel development known as the Commune by the Great Wall.

Looking for building materials locally, Ban discovered that there was little available in wood. What he did find was laminated plywood made from thin strips of bamboo woven into sheets, used as framework for concrete. With help from a bamboo factory he managed to create lumber from laminated bamboo, a construction material with a structural strength between timber and steel. Inspired by traditional Chinese architecture in the remote, rugged landscape, Ban situated his low-slung building around a main courtyard, with all rooms placed around in a simple square footprint. Ban's design is based on what he calls the "furniture system": using pre-fabricated, insulated components for the main structure as well as the interior and exterior walls. But he is convinced that the future of laminated bamboo as a building material "has a great prospect".

Den japanischen Architekten Shigeru Ban erwarteten ein paar Überraschungen, als er zu den zwölf ausgewählten Architekten gehörte, die eines der Häuser für das experimentelle Hotelprojekt unter dem Namen »Commune by the Great Wall« bauen sollten.

Als Ban sich an Ort und Stelle nach Baumaterial aus Holz umsah, war nur wenig vorhanden. Dafür entdeckte er ein Schichtholz aus dünnen, übereinander verleimten Bambusstreifen, die als Verschalung für Beton genutzt wurden. Mit Hilfe einer Bambusfabrik entwickelte er ein Bambus-Schichtholz, das als Baumaterial eine Druckfestigkeit zwischen Holz und Stahl erreicht. Ban ließ sich von der traditionellen chinesischen Architektur und der rauen abgelegenen Landschaft inspirieren und baute sein niedriges Gebäude so um einen zentralen Innenhof herum, dass alle quadratischen Zimmer gleichmäßig darum gruppiert sind. Bei seinem Entwurf wandte er das von ihm so genannte Prinzip des »Furniture System« (Möbelsystems) an, bei dem er sowohl zunächst das Grundgerüst, als dann auch die Aussen- und die Innenwände aus dem vorfabrizierten, dämmenden Material baute, dabei jeweils die einzelnen Elementen einfach zusammensetzte. Shigeru Ban ist inzwischen davon überzeugt, dass dem Bambus als Baumaterial eine große Zukunft bevorsteht.

Invité, avec onze autres architectes, à participer au projet hôtelier expérimental connu sous le nom de Commune de la Grande Muraille, le Japonais Shigeru Ban s'est vu confronté à quelques surprises.

En cherchant des matériaux de construction sur place, Ban s'est aperçu que les ressources en bois se limitaient à des panneaux de contreplaqué obtenus par tissage de bandes de bambou. A partir de ce contreplaqué utilisé à l'origine pour le coffrage du béton, il a mis au point, avec le concours d'une usine de transformation du bambou, un produit stratifié dont la résistance aux contraintes se situe entre celle du bois de construction et celle de l'acier. Puisant son inspiration dans l'architecture traditionnelle de cette région et retirée, Ban a créé une construction basse organisée autour d'une cour principale selon une trame quadrangulaire. Ce projet repose sur ce que Ban appelle le système du « Furniture System » (Système du meuble) : les éléments préfabriqués et isolés thermiquement mis en œuvre servent tant de structure porteuse que d'enveloppe intérieure et extérieure. Il est convaincu que le stratifié de bambou est promis à un bel avenir dans le domaine de la construction.

FACING PAGE Shigeru Ban mainly used lumber made of laminated bamboo for the structure of the house. Interior and exterior walls were also made from pre-fabricated, modular sheets of laminated bamboo. **ABOVE** All the rooms are placed around the clear, clean lines of a main courtyard at the centre of the house. ❊ **LINKE SEITE** Als Baumaterial wählte Shigeru Ban hauptsächlich Schichtholz aus Bambus. Auch die Innen- und Außenwände wurden aus vorproduzierten Bambus-Sperrholzplatten errichtet. **OBEN** Alle Zimmer liegen direkt um den zentralen, nüchtern und klar gestalteten Innenhof. ❊ **PAGE DE GAUCHE** Pour le squelette du bâtiment, Shigeru Ban a recouru presque exclusivement à du stratifié de bambou. Des panneaux de stratifié de bambou habillent la structure. **CI-DESSUS** Toutes les pièces donnent sur une cour centrale aux lignes pures et sobres.

LEONARDO GRIGLIE

BeiJing

An imperial Buddhist temple reincarnated.

Zhu Mu Lang Ma means "Mount Everest" in Chinese. It is the name given to a complex of courtyard houses and temples that date from the Qing dynasty in the 1850s.

They were the last emperor Pu Yi's ancestral temples but fell into disuse with the rise of the Communists. Later the temples were converted into a residence for Tibetan officials. Leonardo Griglie, a journalist-turned-entrepreneur from Piemont who has lived in Asia for many years, came across an abandoned building in the complex – essentially one large empty room – in 1997. It was a minor temple that once served as adjunct to the main shrine. Possessed by a fear of ending up in a small suburban apartment, Griglie hired a young Italian architect to help create a space reminiscent of "a loft and an Italian piazza". A devoted collector of modern Chinese art, Griglie has built a stage set of faux walls and a spiral staircase to preserve the original Qing dynasty ceiling, on facing page, with its imperial dragon design in blue and gold. Fusing the modern with the classical, his bachelor's pad is a modern temple to living in style.

Zhu Mu Lang Ma bedeutet auf Chinesisch »Mount Everest«. So heißt der Gebäudekomplex mit Hofhäusern und Tempeln aus der Zeit der Qing-Dynastie in den 1850er Jahren.

Hier lagen die den Vorfahren geweihten Tempel des letzten Kaisers Pu Yi, die nach der Machtergreifung der Kommunisten nicht mehr genutzt wurden. Später dienten sie als Residenz für tibetische Funktionäre. Leonardo Griglie, ein ehemaliger Journalist aus dem Piemont, heute Unternehmer, lebt seit vielen Jahren in Asien und entdeckte 1997 in dem Gesamtkomplex ein verlassenes Gebäude, das nur aus einem einzigen großen Raum bestand. Es handelte sich um einen weniger bedeutenden Tempel, der ursprünglich als Anbau des Hauptschreins diente. Griglie beauftragte einen jungen italienischen Architekten, den Raum in eine Mischung aus »einem Loft und einer italienischen Piazza« zu verwandeln. Der Bauherr, ein leidenschaftlicher Sammler moderner chinesischer Kunst, ließ ein Bühnenbild aus falschen Wänden und einer Wendeltreppe errichten, um die Decke mit dem kaiserlichen Drachen in Blau und Gold zu erhalten (linke Seite), die noch aus der Zeit der Qing stammt. In der Verschmelzung moderner und klassischer Elemente präsentiert sich die Junggesellenapartment als Tempel modernen Lebensstils.

Zhu Mu Lang Ma signifie «mont Everest» en chinois. C'est le nom donné à un ensemble de maisons à cour carrée et de temples construit au milieu du 19e siècle, sous la dynastie des Qing.

Ces temples aux ancêtres appartenant au dernier empereur Puyi, étaient tombés dans l'oubli avec l'avènement du communisme, avant d'être transformés en résidences pour des fonctionnaires tibétains. En 1997, le Piémontais Leonardo Griglie, journaliste devenu entrepreneur qui vit en Asie depuis de nombreuses années, est tombé sur un bâtiment à l'abandon dans Zhu Mu Lang Ma. Ce temple mineur d'une seule pièce servait naguère d'annexe au sanctuaire principal. Terrifié à l'idée de finir ses jours dans un petit appartement de banlieue, Griglie a commandé à un jeune architecte italien un espace qui tienne «du loft et de la piazza». Collectionneur inconditionnel d'art moderne chinois, Griglie a créé un décor de fausses cloisons et un escalier en colimaçon afin de préserver le plafond à caissons Qing d'origine (page de gauche) reconnaissable à son dragon or sur fond bleu. Fusion de la modernité et du classicisme, son appartement de célibataire est un temple au style de vie moderne.

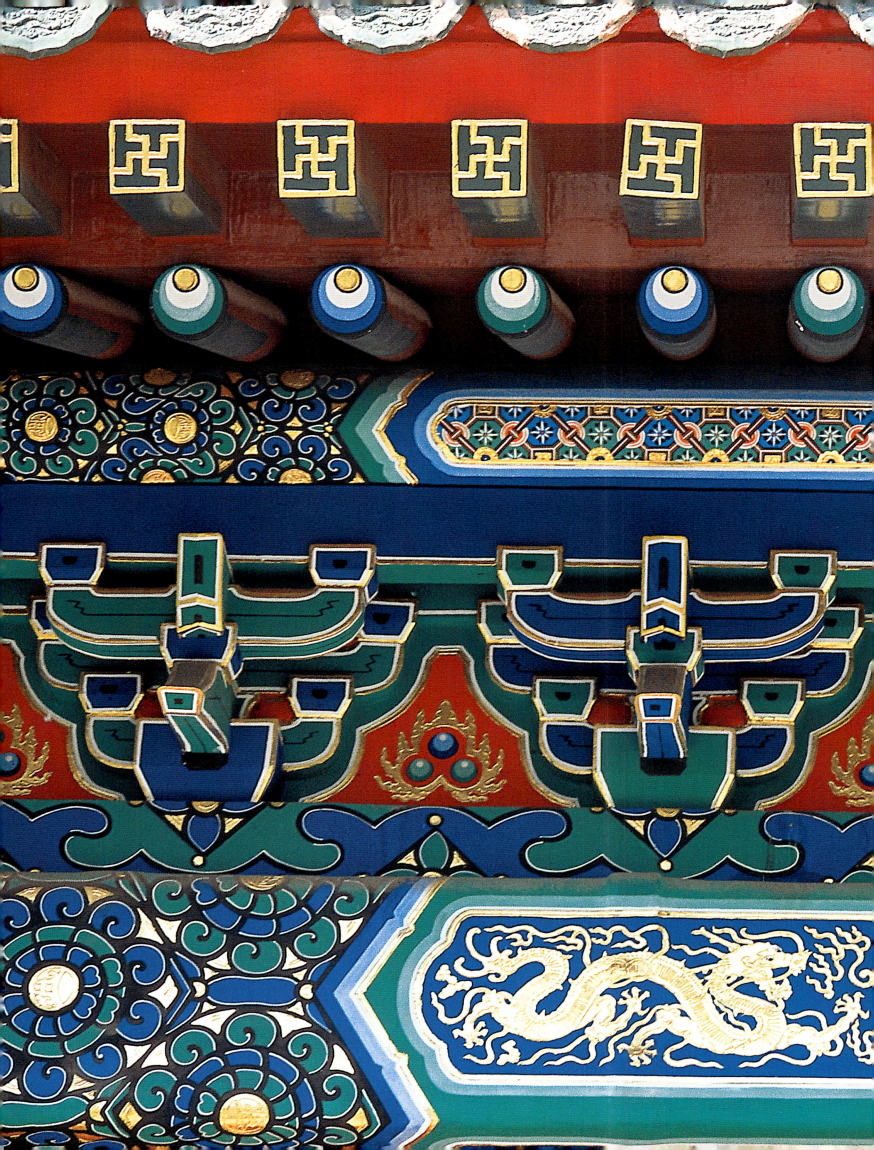

※ **PREVIOUS PAGES** Entrance and views of the roof from the Qing dynasty. Mythical animals on the eaves are symbols of prosperity and good luck. Hanging below the tiles are gilded swastikas, a Buddhist and Hindu religious symbol. Traditional bamboo bird-cages. Detail of the intricately-patterned roof. **ABOVE** The lacquered dining table and chairs are from 1930s Shanghai. On the wall are framed maps of old Beijing. The models of a man and pig in the alcove are acupuncturists' models. **FACING PAGE** Portrait of a youthful Chairman Mao. **FOLLOWING PAGES** a collage of Mao cut-outs of the 1970s. ※ **VORHERGEHENDE DOPPELSEITEN** Eingang und Ansicht vom Dach, das aus der Qing-Periode stammt. Die mythischen Tiere an den Dachtraufen symbolisieren Reichtum und Glück. Unter den Ziegeln hängen vergoldete Swastiken, religiöses Symbol der Hindus und Buddhisten. Traditionelle Vogelkäfige. Detail des kompliziert gemusterten Daches. **OBEN** Der lackierte Esstisch und die Stühle aus den 1930er Jahren stammen aus Shanghai. An der Wand hängen gerahmte Stadtpläne des alten Peking. Die Modelle eines Mannes und eines Schweins in der Nische waren ursprünglich für Akupunkteure gedacht. **RECHTE SEITE** ein Porträt des Vorsitzenden Mao als junger Mann. **FOLGENDE DOPPELSEITE** eine Col-lage aus ausgeschnittenen Mao-Bildern der 1970er Jahre. ※ **DOUBLES PAGES PRECEDENTES** l'entrée et le toit représentatif du style Qing. Les animaux mythiques juchés sur les avant-toits sont des symboles de prospérité et de chance. A l'aplomb du toit, des svastikas dorées, symbole sacré bouddhique et hindouiste. Des cages à oiseaux traditionnelles en bambou sont accrochées dans un plaque-minier. Débauche de motifs et de couleurs sur la toiture aux motifs complexe. **CI-DESSUS** La table et les chaises en laque sont du Shanghai des années 1930. Griglie a fait encadrer des plans du Vieux Pékin. Les écorchés d'homme et de porc présentés dans la niche sont utilisés en acupuncture. **PAGE DE DROITE** un portrait de Mao jeune homme. **DOUBLE PAGE SUIVANTE** un collage de portraits de Mao des années 1970.

JEHANNE DE BIOLLEY AND HARRISON LIU BEIJING

A Belgian bijou in a Ming dynasty setting.

It did not require much persuasion to convert Jehanne de Biolley into an ardent Sinophile. For as long as she can remember the colours, shapes and textures of Asia have fired her imagination, especially during the years when she ran an oriental gallery in London.

When Jehanne moved to Beijing some years ago she instantly felt at home. One problem remained: where to locate a family home for her husband, the Chinese artist Harrison Liu, and their young son Geng Ji? What they found north of the Forbidden City were three decaying 17th-century pavilions around a large courtyard. The house was once a printing factory and school before it fell into disrepair. Jehanne and Harrison have remained faithful to the original spaces in their adaptation: the north pavilion is a living area divided by screens; the west pavilion houses the kitchen and guest room; and the east pavilion is Jehanne's jewellery workshop. Many pieces of furniture were designed by Liu while objects, such as the gramophone and 1950s Chinese opera records on the facing page, were found on Beijing's streets.

Es bedurfte nur wenig, um Jehanne de Biolley in eine leidenschaftliche Verehrerin alles Chinesischen zu verwandeln. Seit jeher animierten die Farben, Formen und Gestalten Asiens ihre Vorstellungskraft, und das bereits, als sie in England eine orientalische Galerie führte.

Als Jehanne vor einigen Jahren nach Peking zog, fühlte sie sich sofort zu Hause. Es gab nur ein Problem: Wo sollte sie mit ihrem Mann, dem chinesischen Künstler Harrison Liu, und dem kleinen Sohn Chen Ji wohnen? Nördlich der Verbotenen Stadt fanden sie schließlich drei baufällige Pavillons aus dem 17. Jahrhundert, die sich um einen großen Hof gruppierten. Bevor es verfiel, residierte eine Druckerei in dem Hofhaus, später eine Schule. Beim Umbau behielten Jehanne und Harrison die ursprüngliche Raumaufteilung bei. Der Wohnbereich im Nordpavillon ist durch Trennwände geteilt, im Westpavillon liegen die Küche und das Gästezimmer, und im Ostpavillon ist Jehannes Goldschmiedewerkstatt untergebracht. Harrison Liu hat viele Möbel entworfen, andere Einrichtungsgegenstände wie das Grammofon und die chinesischen Opernplatten aus den 1950er Jahren (Bild links) fanden sie bei den Straßenhändlern der Stadt.

Il n'a pas fallu insister beaucoup pour faire de Jehanne de Biolley une fervente sinophile. D'aussi loin qu'elle se souvienne, les couleurs, formes et textures d'Asie ont toujours enflammé son imagination, surtout à l'époque où elle dirigeait une galerie asiatique à Londres.

Quand Jehanne s'est installée à Pékin avec son mari, l'artiste chinois Harrison Liu, et leur jeune fils Cheng Ji, il y a quelques années, elle s'y est immédiatement sentie chez elle. Son seul problème était alors de trouver un toit. C'est au nord de la Cité interdite que Jehanne et Harrison ont débusqué trois bâtiments 17e délabrés disposés autour d'une cour. La construction avait abrité une imprimerie puis une école. C'est dans le plus grand respect des bâtiments d'origine qu'ils les ont convertis en habitation : divisé par des paravents, le pavillon nord abrite les pièces de vie, le bâtiment ouest la cuisine et la chambre d'amis, et le bâtiment est l'atelier de bijouterie de Jehanne. De nombreux meubles sont signés Harrison Liu, tandis que divers objets, tels que le gramophone et les enregistrements d'opéra chinois des années 1950 (page de gauche), ont été trouvés en chinant dans les rues de Pékin.

ABOVE Jehanne de Biolley with husband Harrison Liu and son Cheng Ji in their tree-filled courtyard. They are on a typical Beijing tricycle used to ferry people and goods in the city. Hanging from the trees are reproductions of traditional lanterns made of iron wire and wood. ❊ **OBEN** Jehanne de Biolley mit ihrem Mann Harrison Liu und Sohn Cheng Ji in dem baumbestandenen Hof. Das Lastendreirad ist ein alltägliches Fahrzeug, mit dem Menschen und Waren in Peking transportiert werden. Am Baum hängen Nachbildungen traditioneller Laternen aus Eisendraht und Holz. ❊ **CI-DESSUS** Jehanne de Biolley, son mari Harrison Liu et leur fils Cheng Ji dans la cour très arborée. C'est sur ces cyclopousses qu'on transporte personnes et marchandises dans Pékin. Des répliques de lanternes traditionnelles en fil de fer et bois sont accrochées dans les arbres.

ABOVE a view of the courtyard from the corridor connecting the west and north pavilions of the house. The red-painted wood railings and window frames are traditional. ✳ **OBEN** Blick auf den Innenhof von dem Gang aus, der den West- und den Nordpavillon des Hauses miteinander verbindet. Die rot gestrichenen Geländer und Fensterrahmen aus Holz entsprechen der Tradition. ✳ **CI-DESSUS** la cour vue du corridor reliant les pavillons ouest et nord de la maison. Les rambardes et châssis de fenêtre peintes en rouge sont traditionnels.

PREVIOUS PAGES, FROM TOP LEFT A malachite and enamel necklace designed by Jehanne de Biolley is draped on a glazed pottery sculpture of mother and child. The green leather sofas in the living room date from the 1970s. The woollen carpet is from Xinjiang. The painting above the Chinese altar table is by Harrison Liu. The living room's wooden columns are lacquered a deep red. ABOVE The bronze bed in the bedroom was designed by Harrison Liu. The bedspread and cushions are of silk trimmed with velvet, gold brocade and satin. LEFT A necklace designed by Jehanne made of coral, turquoise and red Chinese seeds. FACING PAGE Lacquer boxes with ceramic vases stand beside an antique wooden screen lined with red and gold brocade. ❋ VORHERGEHENDE DOPPELSEITE VON LINKS OBEN Eine Kette aus Malachit und Email nach einem Entwurf von Jehanne de Biolley liegt dekorativ über einer glasierten Mutter-Kind-Keramikskulptur. Die grünen Ledersofas im Wohnzimmer stammen aus den 1970er Jahren. Der Wollteppich wurde in der autonomen Region Xinjiang geknüpft. Harrison Liu malte das Bild über dem chinesischen Altar. Die Holzsäulen im Wohnzimmer sind dunkelrot lackiert. OBEN Harrison Liu entwarf das Bronzebett im Schlafzimmer. Die Tagesdecke und die Kissen sind aus mit Samt, Goldbrokat und Satin besetzter Seide. LINKS Jehanne entwarf eine Kette aus roten Korallen und Türkis. RECHTE SEITE Die Lackkisten mit den Keramikvasen stehen neben einer antiken Trennwand aus Holz, die mit von Rot und Gold durchwirktem Brokat bezogen ist. ❋ DOUBLE PAGE PRECEDENTE, À PARTIR D'EN HAUT À GAUCHE Un collier en malachite et émaux créé par Jehanne de Biolley pare une sculpture de « mère à l'enfant » en poterie vernissée. Les sofas en cuir vert datent des années 1970. Le tapis de laine provient de Xinjiang. Le tableau accroché au-dessus de la table chinoise est signé Harrison Liu. Des colonnes de bois laquées dans un rouge profond rythment le salon. CI-DESSUS Harrison Liu a dessiné le lit en bronze de la chambre à coucher. Le dessus de lit et les coussins sont en soie bordée de velours, brocarts d'or et satin. A GAUCHE une création de Jehanne, en corail et turquoise. PAGE DE DROITE Des vases en céramique exposés sur des boîtes en laque se détachent sur le fond d'un paravent ancien tendu de brocart rouge et or.

PASCALE DESVAUX
BEiJing

Chinese symbols of happiness.

Pascale Desvaux trained as an architect in France and came to live in Beijing with her husband and three children five years ago. Two things immediately gripped her: a desire to live in a traditional courtyard house and, within its precincts, explore the interconnection of spaces.

Desvaux became fascinated by concepts of enclosure and separation in Chinese architecture. Brought up with a preference for contemporary design and its clear, simple lines, she found that her personal style became eclectic. Moon gates became a lingering motif in her renovation of an old house. Inspired by the red-painted garden gates, she decided to link interior spaces with deep blue moon gates. They were both unconventional and functional in a house made up of separate wings. Equally original is the way she has decorated her house: in a stylish mélange of flea market finds, brand names in European furniture, Chinese antiques and self-designed pieces. The courtyard house offers an entirely original take on the Chinese principle of a home as a heavenly abode.

Pascale Desvaux arbeitete als Architektin in Frankreich und zog vor fünf Jahren mit ihrem Mann und drei Kindern nach Peking. Von Anfang an hatte sie zwei Ziele: in einem traditionellen Hofhaus zu wohnen und auf dem angrenzenden Gelände die Verbindung von Räumen zu erforschen.

Konzepte zur räumlichen Umschließung und Trennung in der chinesischen Architektur üben eine große Faszination auf Desvaux aus. Obwohl sie zu einer Vorliebe für zeitgenössisches Design und dessen klare, einfache Linienführung erzogen worden ist, stellte sich ihr eigener Stil als durchaus eklektizistisch heraus. Bei der Renovierung eines alten Hauses setzte sie auf Mondtore als Leitmotiv. Sie ließ sich von den rot gestrichenen Gartentoren inspirieren und beschloss, auch die Innenräume untereinander mit Mondtoren zu verbinden. In dem mehrflügeligen Haus wirken sie so unkonventionell wie zweckmäßig. Nicht weniger originell richtete die Eigentümerin die Räume ein: Sie schuf eine kunstvolle Mischung aus Flohmarktschnäppchen, europäischen Markenmöbeln, chinesischen Antiquitäten und selbst entworfenen Objekten. Das Hofhaus entpuppt sich als ungewöhnliche Interpretation der chinesischen Vorstellung eines himmlischen Wohnsitzes.

Après des études d'architecture en France, Pascale Desvaux s'est installée à Pékin avec son mari et ses trois enfants il y a cinq ans. Elle a aussitôt eu envie de vivre dans une maison traditionnelle à cour intérieure et d'y explorer les relations entre les espaces.

Cette architecte est fascinée par les concepts d'espace clos et séparés dans l'architecture chinoise. Ayant, de par son éducation, une nette préférence pour le style contemporain et ses lignes claires et nettes, elle a vu son style personnel glisser vers l'éclectisme. Les portes en forme de pleine lune sont un motif-clé dans la vieille maison qu'elle a rénovée. Inspirée par les portes peintes en rouge du jardin, elle a décidé de faire communiquer les espaces intérieurs entre eux par des portes circulaires bleu nuit, solution non conventionnelle mais fonctionnelle dans une maison constituée de corps de bâtiments indépendants. La décoration intérieure de la maison est tout aussi originale: avec beaucoup de goût, elle marie objets dénichés aux Puces, meubles de marque européens, antiquités chinoises et créations personnelles. Cette maison est une adaptation tout à fait originale de la vision chinoise de la maison en tant que demeure céleste.

FACING PAGE moon gate entrance in the outer wall of the courtyard. The colour red represents happiness and prosperity. A blue moon gate leads from the living room into the kitchen. The table top is of specially treated bricks, commonly used as flooring. **ABOVE** moon gate leading to the bedroom. The statue on the bedside table was bought from a roadside stall. The colonial chair was custom-made. ❊ **LINKE SEITE** der Eingang durch ein Mondtor an der Außenmauer des Hofes. Die rote Farbe symbolisiert Glück und Wohlstand. Ein blaues Mondtor führt vom Wohnzimmer in die Küche. Die Tischoberfläche besteht aus speziell behandelten Ziegeln, die normalerweise für Böden benutzt werden. **OBEN** Das Mondtor führt ins Schlafzimmer. Die Skulptur auf dem Nachttisch stammt von einem Straßenhändler. Der Stuhl im Kolonialstil wurde eigens angefertigt. ❊ **PAGE DE GAUCHE** Une porte d'entrée circulaire a été ménagée dans le mur fermant la cour. Le rouge est symbole de bonheur et prospérité. Une porte circulaire bleue entre le salon et la cuisine. Le plateau de la table est en briques traitées, généralement utilisées comme revêtement de sol. **CI-DESSUS** La porte donne sur la chambre. La statue sur la table de chevet provient d'un vide-grenier. Le fauteuil de style colonial a été fabriqué sur mesure.

BELOW A traditional wooden bed is used as a sofa. **FACING PAGE** detail of a silk print on a Chinese lantern showing Ming dynasty figures. ✷ **UNTEN** Das traditionelle Bett wurde in ein Sofa verwandelt. **RECHTE SEITE** Das auf Seide gedruckte Motiv auf einer chinesischen Laterne präsentiert Figuren aus der Ming-Dynastie. ✷ **CI-DESSOUS** un lit traditionnel en bois recyclé en sofa. **PAGE DE DROITE** une lanterne chinoise tendue de soie imprimée ; les personnages sont un motif typique du style Ming.

FACING PAGE traditional lanterns made from paper and wire mesh. The Chinese character stands for good luck. ABOVE Chairs dating from the Cultural Revolution. FOLLOWING PAGES an assortment of birdcages picked up in local markets. ✳ LINKE SEITE traditionelle Laternen aus Papier und Drahtgeflecht. Das chinesische Schriftzeichen bedeutet Glück. OBEN Die Stühle stammen aus der Zeit der Kulturrevolution. FOLGENDE DOPPELSEITEN Die Besitzer erwarben die Vogelkäfig-Sammlung auf verschiedenen Märkten. ✳ PAGE DE GAUCHE des lanternes traditionnelles en papier et grillage. Le caractère chinois signifie bonheur. CI-DESSUS des fauteuils datant de la Révolution culturelle. DOUBLE PAGE SUIVANTE Les cages à oiseaux proviennent de marchés locaux.

THE RED CAPITAL RESIDENCE

Beijing

A nostalgic period piece.

Memories of Edgar Snow, Han Suyin and Henry Kissinger have all gone into creating a flashback of China's modern history in the Red Capital Club and Residence.

It all began when New York-born lawyer and investment analyst Laurence Brahm spent two decades opening doors for multinationals in China. He became taken by the idea of architecture as an expression of people's environment and psychology; when he came upon a courtyard house in Beijing's heritage Dongsi district his task seemed cut out. What started as a club has now grown into a five-roomed residence nearby, each suite styled after a particular personage or period. There is the Chairman's Suite after Mao's life and times, two courtyards inspired by concubines and two more that evoke the romantic, revolutionary times of Han Suyin and Edgar Snow. "We would gather in the evenings in the raftered hall of some old Peking mansion…the girls in flowered dresses…with flowers in their hair," sighed Han Suyin. Whimsical and delightfully distracting, it is a period piece captured in a rare style.

Erinnerungen an Edgar Snow, Han Suyin und Henry Kissinger flossen ein in die Rückschau auf Chinas moderne Geschichte bei der Gestaltung der »Red Capital Club and Residence«.

Das Unternehmen begann damit, dass Rechtsanwalt und Börsenanalyst Laurence Brahm zwei Jahrzehnte lang als Türöffner für internationale Firmen in China fungierte. Er war fasziniert von der Architektur als Ausdruck von Kultur und Lebensbedürfnissen der Menschen, und als er das Hofhaus in Pekings altem Bezirk Dongsi entdeckte, wusste er sofort, was er zu tun hatte. Zunächst gab es nur den Club, der sich inzwischen zu einer Anlage mit fünf Zimmern entwickelt hat. Jede Suite wurde nach einer besonderen Person oder Epoche eingerichtet – es gibt eine »Chairman's Suite«, die sich auf Maos Leben und Historie bezieht, zwei Innenhöfe, die von Konkubinen inspiriert wurden, sowie zwei weitere, die jene romantischen revolutionären Zeiten eines Han Suyin und eines Edgar Snow beschwören. Han Suyin erinnerte sich mit einem Seufzer: »Damals versammelten wir uns unter dem alten Gebälk eines Saals in einem alten Pekinger Herrenhaus … die Mädchen in Blümchenkleidern … mit Blüten im Haar.« – Club und Residenz präsentieren sich als außergewöhnliches Stück Zeitgeschichte, das einen unterhaltsamen Charme ganz eigener Art verbreitet.

Des souvenirs d'Edgar Snow, Han Suyin et Henry Kissinger ont été exploités pour créer les Red Capital Club et Residence, qui reflètent l'histoire moderne de la Chine.

Laurence Brahm, un avocat et expert en placements new-yorkais, s'est employé pendant une vingtaine d'années à ouvrir le marché chinois aux multinationales. Un jour, il a pris conscience du fait que l'architecture est l'expression de la psychologie des gens et des conditions naturelles et culturelles qui règnent en un lieu. Un peu plus tard, il a trouvé à Pékin une maison à cour carrée dans le quartier historique de Dongsi, et une grande aventure a commencé. Ce qui n'était au début qu'un club a été doté d'une résidence comportant cinq suites consacrées à un personnage particulier ou à une époque donnée. La suite du Grand Timonier reprend des éléments de la vie de Mao et de son temps. Deux cours ont été inspirées par des concubines et deux autres évoquent les époques romantiques et révolutionnaires de Han Suyin et Edgar Snow. «Le soir, nous nous retrouvions dans la salle à poutres apparentes de quelque vieille demeure de Pékin … les jeunes filles dans leurs robes à fleurs … avec des fleurs dans les cheveux», soupirait Han Suyin. Etrange et délicieusement dépaysante, cette résidence est la reproduction nostalgique d'une époque.

ABOVE The entrance courtyard apes the style of residence favoured by the Communist elite after 1949. **BELOW** A vintage red-flagged limo used by Mao's widow is parked outside the courtyard. ❊ **OBEN** Der Eingangshof ist im Stil jener Herrenhäuser, die von der kommunistischen Elite nach 1949 bevorzugt wurden, gehalten. **UNTEN** Die Oldtimer-Limousine mit roten Fähnchen – sie gehörte Mao's Witwe – parkt vor dem Hof. ❊ **CI-DESSUS** La première cour imite le style de résidence en faveur auprès de l'élite communiste après 1949. **CI-DESSOUS** Une limousine de collection arborant le drapeau rouge – elle appartient à la veuve de Mao – est garée contre le mur d'enceinte.

ABOVE A hidden passage under the rock garden leads to a bar that was a bomb shelter built in 1969 on Marshal Lin Biao's orders. BELOW A typical Beijing trishaw ferries guests from the Red Capital Residence to the Red Capital Club nearby. ※ OBEN Ein unterirdischer Gang unter dem Steingarten führt zu einer Bar, die ursprünglich 1969 unter Marschall Lin Biao als Bunker erbaut worden war. UNTEN Eine charakteristische dreirädrigte Rikscha bringt die Gäste von der »Red Capital Residence« zum nahe gelegenen »Red Capital Club«. ※ CI-DESSUS Un passage dérobé sous le jardin de pierres mène au bar, un ancien abri antiaérien construit en 1969 par ordre du maréchal Lin Biao. CI-DESSOUS Ce cyclopousse pékinois typique fait la navette entre la « Red Capital Residence » et le « Red Capital Club » situé à proximité.

东方红
——毛泽东画典

FACING PAGE A book with Chairman Mao on the cover graces the library and cigar lounge of the Red Capital Club amidst other Mao-era memorabilia. **ABOVE** A detachment of staff in Maoist uniform greets guests at the door. ❋ **LINKE SEITE** Inmitten weiterer Mao-Devotionalien ziert ein Buch über den Vorsitzenden Mao die Bibliothek und Zigarren-Lounge des »Red Capital Club«. **OBEN** Eine Abordnung des Personals in maoistischer Uniform begrüßt die Gäste an der Tür. ❋ **PAGE DE GAUCHE** Parmi d'autres souvenirs de l'ère de Mao, un livre avec le Grand Timonier sur la couverture orne la bibliothèque et le fumoir du « Red Capital Club ». **CI-DESSUS** Une employée en tenue maoïste accueille les visiteurs à la porte.

ABOVE The Chairman's Suite pays tribute to a collection of popular Mao-period bric-a-brac. FACING PAGE The lounge of the Red Capital Residence is decorated in the style of Mao's private library. ❋ OBEN In der Suite, die dem Vorsitzenden Mao gewidmet ist, zollt ihm eine Nippes-Sammlung Tribut. RECHTE SEITE Die Lounge der »Red Capital Residence« kopiert stilistisch Maos Privatbibliothek. ❋ CI-DESSUS La suite du Grand Timonier recèle une collection de bibelots en vogue à son époque. PAGE DE DROITE La décoration du salon de la « Red Capital Residence » est inspirée de la bibliothèque privée de Mao.

ABOVE Each bathroom in the Red Capital Residence is a romantic adaptation of China's Republican era. **FACING PAGE** The bed in the "West Concubine's Suite" is a genuine Qing dynasty piece, from the period when Emperor Tongzhi and the Dowager Empress Ci Xi ruled from the Forbidden City. ❀ **OBEN** Alle Badezimmer in der »Red Capital Residence« erinnern auf romantische Art und Weise an die Republik China. **RECHTE SEITE** Das Bett in der »West Concubine Suite« stammt aus jener Epoche der Qing-Dynastie, als Kaiser Tongzhi und die Kaiserwitwe Cixi in der Verbotenen Stadt herrschten. ❀ **CI-DESSUS** Chaque salle de bains de la « Red Capital Residence » évoque de manière romantique la république de Chine. **PAGE DE DROITE** Le lit de la suite de la concubine de l'Ouest est un authentique meuble Qing, de l'époque où l'empereur Tongzhi et sa mère l'impératrice douairière Cixi régnaient sur la Cité interdite.

THE CHINA CLUB

BEIJING

Luxury puts on royal gloves.

When David Tang launched the second of his China Clubs in Beijing in 1996, the turnout was impressive. Among the celebrities who flew in to attend were Kevin Costner, the Duchess of York and Michael Caine.

The club is situated in a small 17th-century palace near Tiananmen Square that once belonged to a prince descended from Emperor Kangxi of the Qing dynasty. For 37 years the complex, made up of four courtyards and surrounded by interconnected pavilions, was occupied by the best Sichuan restaurant in town, a place frequently patronized by the Chinese leader Deng Xiao Ping. Extensive renovation and careful refurbishing were undertaken by Tang to return the buildings to their princely glory. A three-storeyed Chinese pavilion was added in 1998; it now houses several members' suites as well as the Sichuan Pavilion, a speciality restaurant. From small parlours for private dining to larger banqueting facilities, Beijing's China Club also includes the Long March Bar, a hallmark of China Clubs elsewhere. The quiet lane in the heart of the bustling capital now houses a perfectly-restored oasis.

Als David Tang 1996 seinen zweiten China Club in Peking eröffnete, wurde das gebührend gefeiert. Zur Eröffnung kamen Stars wie Kevin Costner, die Herzogin von York und Michael Caine.

Der Club liegt nahe des Tien'anmen-Platzes in einem kleinen Palast aus dem 17. Jahrhundert, einst Besitz eines Prinzen, der von Kaiser Kangxi aus der Qing-Dynastie abstammte. 37 Jahre lang war in dem Gebäudekomplex aus vier Innenhöfen und miteinander verbundenen Pavillons das beste Sichuan-Restaurant der Stadt beheimatet, das auch der chinesische Politiker Deng Xiaoping häufig beehrte. Tang ließ die Gebäude renovieren und mit ausgesuchten Möbeln ausstatten, um den Palast erneut in prinzlichem Glanz erstrahlen zu lassen. 1998 wurde ein dreistöckiger chinesischer Pavillon angebaut, in dem heute die Suiten einiger Clubmitglieder sowie der »Sichuan Pavillon«, ein Spezialitätenrestaurant, untergebracht sind. Der China Club in Peking ist für alle Gelegenheiten ausgestattet und bietet von kleinen Salons für intime Abendeinladungen bis zu großen Bankettsälen die passenden Räumlichkeiten. Selbstverständlich gibt es auch eine »Bar des langen Marsches«, das Wahrzeichen aller China Clubs. In der stillen Straße im Zentrum der geschäftigen Hauptstadt residiert jetzt eine perfekt restaurierte Oase der Gastlichkeit.

Lorsque David Tang a ouvert son deuxième China Club à Pékin en 1996, les célébrités y ont afflué, parmi lesquelles Kevin Costner, la duchesse d'York et Michael Caine.

Situé à proximité de la place Tiananmen, ce club est installé dans un petit palais du 17e siècle qui a appartenu à un prince, descendant de l'empereur Kangxi, de la dynastie des Qing. 37 ans durant, cet ensemble de quatre cours entourées de pavillons communiquant entre eux a hébergé le meilleur restaurant de cuisine séchuanaise de la ville, et le chef d'Etat Deng Xiaoping y avait ses habitudes. Tang a rénové en profondeur et réaménagé avec beaucoup de soin les bâtiments pour leur rendre leur lustre passé. Ajouté en 1998, un pavillon chinois de deux étages abrite plusieurs suites réservées aux membres du club ainsi que le restaurant « Sichuan Pavilion ». Outre les petits salons particuliers et les salles réservées aux banquets, le China Club de Pékin comprend un « Bar de la Longue Marche », comme tous les autres China Clubs. Cette rue tranquille au cœur de la capitale trépidante recèle désormais une oasis restaurée à la perfection.

PREVIOUS PAGES views of the China Club's courtyards and the "Sichuan Pavilion". ABOVE an antique standing lamp outside one of the six private dining rooms. FACING PAGE Stone lions guard the entrance from evil spirits. ✳ VORHERGEHENDE DOPPELSEITEN Blick in die Innenhöfe des Clubgeländes und auf den »Sichuan Pavillon«. OBEN eine antike Stehlampe vor einem der sechs privaten Speisesalons. RECHTE SEITE Steinerne Löwen schützen den Eingang vor bösen Geistern. ✳ DOUBLE PAGE PRECEDENTE vue sur les cours intérieures du club et sur le « Sichuan Pavillon ». CI-DESSUS un lampadaire chinois ancien à la porte d'un des six salons particuliers. PAGE DE DROITE Une paire de lions de pierre barrent le passage aux esprits malveillants.

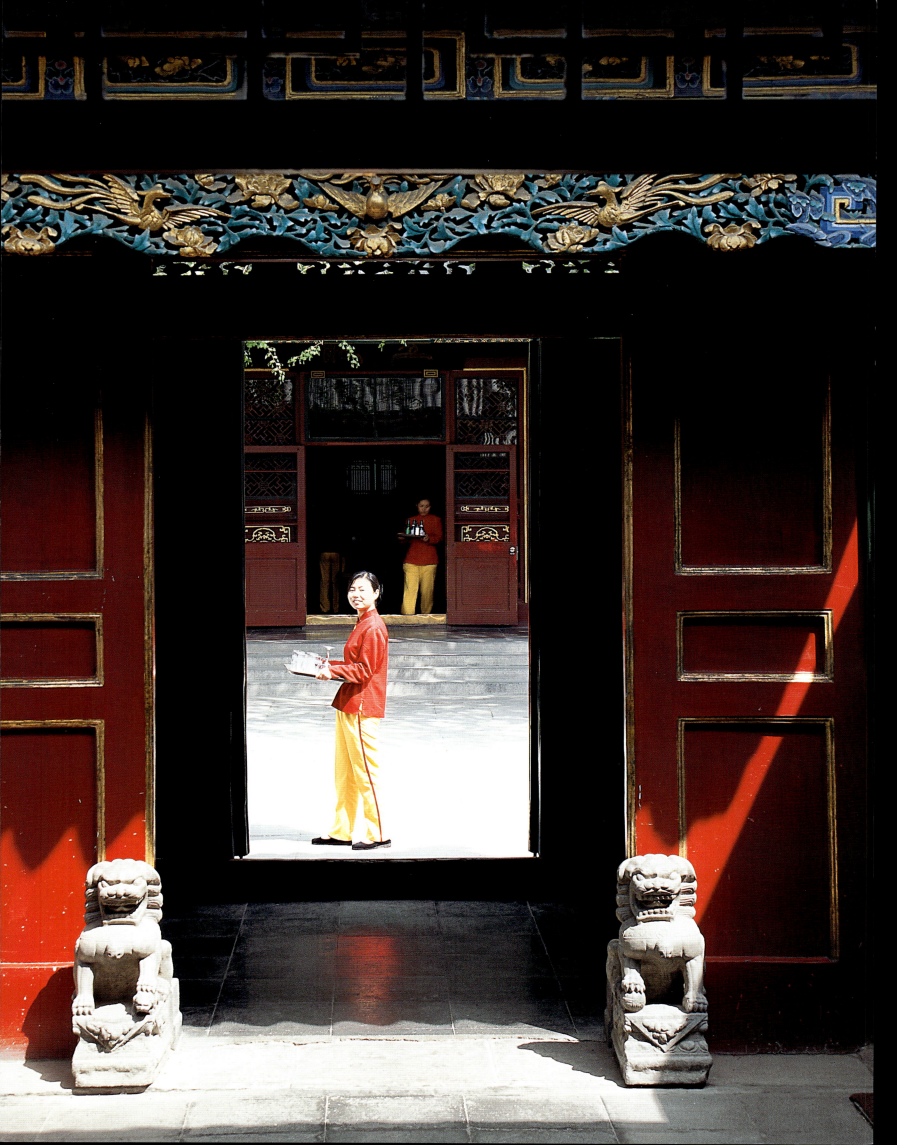

ABOVE Tall lattice doors lined with white cotton blinds divide the bedroom from the living area in a guest suite. ❋ **OBEN** Hohe Gittertüren mit weißen Baumwollrollos schirmen das Schlafzimmer vom Wohnbereich der Gästesuite ab. ❋ **CI-DESSUS** Dans cette suite, des portes à claire-voie tendues de rideaux de coton blanc séparent la chambre du salon.

ABOVE comfortable red chairs in the living area of a guest suite. The silk lampshades were made famous by Chinese film-maker Zhang Yimou in his film "Raise the Red Lantern". ❋ **OBEN** bequeme rote Sessel im Wohnbereich einer Gästesuite. Die seidenen Lampenschirme wurden durch Zhang Yimous Film »Die rote Laterne« berühmt. ❋ **CI-DESSUS** Les sofas rouges dans le salon d'une suite invitent à la détente. Les abat-jour en soie ont été mis au goût du jour par « Epouses et Concubines », film de Zhang Yimou.

FACING PAGE a corner of a Ming-style private dining room near the second courtyard. The China Club's dinner service is in green and white. ABOVE another private dining corner viewed through a carved moon gate. BELOW A Business cards rack of Beijing's hot spots near the reception counter of the Sichuan Pavilion. ※ LINKE SEITE eine Ecke des im Ming-Stil eingerichteten privaten Speisesalons unweit des zweiten Hofes. Das Abendservice des China Club ist in Grün und Weiß gehalten. OBEN Durch ein holzgeschnitztes Mondtor blickt man in einen weiteren privaten Speiseraum. UNTEN ein Ständer mit Visitenkarten aller angesagten Adressen in Peking an der Rezeption des »Sichuan Pavillon«. ※ PAGE DE GAUCHE Le salon particulier de style Ming donne sur la deuxième cour. Le service de table de ce China Club est vert et blanc. CI-DESSUS un autre salon particulier dans l'encadrement d'une porte circulaire en bois sculpté. CI-DESSOUS toutes les bonnes adresses de Pékin dans un casier, à la réception du « Sichuan Pavillon ».

THE FORBIDDEN CITY
City
BeiJing

A walk into the home of the "Son of Heaven".

For 500 years ordinary mortals could not enter the seat of the emperors of China. Today, thousands of tourists throng its courtyards, sipping coffee and shopping for souvenirs in several minor buildings.

Built between 1407 and 1420 by Yongle, the third Ming emperor, 14 Ming and 10 Qing dynasty emperors ruled from the Forbidden City, until the last "Son of Heaven" was driven out in 1924. About a million workers and thousands of artisans were put to hard labour to complete the world's largest palace. It covers 74 hectares and is surrounded by a six-metre deep moat and a ten-metre high wall. In its heyday, life inside was fraught with intrigue, rigid protocol and damage from earthquake and fire, often sparked by firework displays or conniving eunuchs and officials. Much of the decoration visible dates from the 18th century. In the 20th century, Japanese forces and the Kuomintang looted many of its treasures. But enough of the splendour remains, from the imperial yellow roof tiles to the symmetries of scale: courtyard upon courtyard leading to the hidden heart of absolute power.

Normalsterbliche durften den Sitz des Kaisers von China 500 Jahre lang nicht betreten. Heutzutage strömen die Touristen durch die Innenhöfe, trinken Kaffee und erwerben Souvenirs in den weniger bedeutenden Gebäuden der Verbotenen Stadt.

14 Ming- und zehn Qing-Dynastien herrschten von der Verbotenen Stadt aus, die in der Zeit von 1407 bis 1420 unter Yongle, dem dritten Ming-Kaiser erbaut wurde. Der letzte »Himmelssohn« musste 1924 abdanken. Zur Vollendung des größten Palastes der Welt trugen in Schwerstarbeit eine Million Arbeiter und tausende von Handwerkern bei. Ein sechs Meter tiefer Wassergraben und eine zehn Meter hohe Mauer umgeben den Palast, der sich über 74 Hektar erstreckt. Zu seinen Glanzzeiten war das Leben in der Verbotenen Stadt von Intrigen und strengem Protokoll bestimmt, aber auch Erdbeben und Feuer, deren Ursache oft Feuerwerksvorführungen oder Brandstiftung durch verschwörerische Eunuchen und Funktionäre waren. Was heute vom Dekor erhalten ist, stammt zum größten Teil aus dem 18. Jahrhundert. Japanische Truppen und die Kuomintang plünderten im 20. Jahrhundert den Palast. Doch viel von der ehemaligen Pracht ist noch zu erkennen – von den Dachziegeln in kaiserlichem Gelb bis zur allgegenwärtigen Symmetrie: Eine schier unendliche Abfolge von Innenhöfen führt ins versteckte Herz der uneingeschränkten Macht.

Pendant un demi millénaire, le commun des mortels n'eut pas le droit de pénétrer dans la résidence des empereurs de Chine. De nos jours des hordes de touristes se pressent dans ses cours, ses cafés et ses boutiques de souvenirs.

Construite entre 1407 et 1420 par Yong-Lo, le troisième empereur de la dynastie Ming, la Cité interdite a été la résidence de 14 empereurs Ming et dix empereurs Qing, jusqu'à l'expulsion du dernier Fils du Ciel en 1924. Environ un million d'ouvriers et des milliers d'artisans ont péniblement mené à bien la construction de ce qui allait être le plus grand palais au monde, couvrant 74 hectares et entouré par un mur de dix mètres de hauteur et de douves de six mètres de profondeur. A son heure de gloire, la Cité interdite était régentée par un protocole rigide et vivait au rythme des intrigues, des tremblements de terre et incendies, souvent provoqués par des feux d'artifice ou des eunuques de connivence avec des mandarins. La majeure partie de la décoration encore visible date du 18e siècle. Malgré les pillages perpétrés par l'armée japonaise et le Guomindang au 20e siècle, la Cité interdite a gardé une grande partie de sa splendeur, des tuiles jaune impérial à l'enfilade de cours toujours plus petites menant au cœur caché du pouvoir absolu.

PREVIOUS PAGES, CLOCKWISE FROM TOP LEFT A bronze cauldron in a courtyard was used to store water to quench fires. A white marble balustrade leads to an inner court. The central ramp is carved with a pattern of dragons and clouds. Mythical and real animals on upturned eaves were meant to ward off evil. an entrance gate to a courtyard. **ABOVE** The emperor's throne room from where he conducted his administration. **BELOW** A young visitor finds a restful spot under a statue of a protective guardian lion. **FACING PAGE** Guardian lions are placed at six entrances in the Forbidden City. ❈ **VORHERGEHENDE DOPPELSEITEN, IM UHRZEIGERSINN VON LINKS OBEN** Der Bronzekessel in einem der Innenhöfe diente früher als Behälter für Löschwasser. Eine weiße Balustrade führt zu einem Innenhof. Ein Muster aus Drachen und Wolken ziert die Rampe in der Mitte. Mythische und echte Tiere auf aufgerichteten Dachtraufen sollten das Böse abwehren. Ein Eingangstor zu einem Hof. **OBEN** Der Thronsaal des Kaisers, der von hier aus sein Reich verwaltete. **UNTEN** Ein junger Besucher ruht sich unter der Skulptur eines schützenden Löwen aus. **RECHTE SEITE** Weibliche und männliche Löwen aus Stein und vergoldeter Bronze schützen die sechs Eingänge der Verbotenen Stadt. ❈ **DOUBLE PAGE PRECEDENTE, DANS LE SENS DES AIGUILLES D'UNE MONTRE, À PARTIR D'EN HAUT À GAUCHE** Dans ce chaudron de bronze, on stockait de l'eau dans la cour pour éteindre les incendies. L'escalier en marbre blanc conduit à une cour intérieure. Des dragons et des nuages sont sculptés dans la rampe centrale. Les animaux, mythiques ou réels, qui ornent cet avant-toit incurvé étaient censés éloigner le mal. La porte d'entrée d'une cour. **CI-DESSUS** la salle du trône, siège du pouvoir impérial. **CI-DESSOUS** Un jeune visiteur a trouvé une cachette entre les pattes d'une statue de lion. **ET PAGE DE DROITE** Des lions et lionnes de pierre ou de bronze doré veillent devant les six portes de la Cité interdite.

THE GRAND HYATT
SHANGHAI

A dizzy dazzler
for the Guinness Book of Records.

If hotels were mountains then the Grand Hyatt in Shanghai would count as the Mount Everest of the hospitality industry. It made it to the millennium edition of the Guinness Book of Records as the highest hotel in the world.

Located between the 53rd and 87th floors of the 88-storey Jin Mao Tower, the 555-room hotel commands spectacular views over the glittering spread of modern Shanghai. The river Huangpu bisects the city into two parts, Pudong to the east and Puxi to the west. The Grand Hyatt lies in the heart of Pudong, Shanghai's financial district with its monumental towers thrusting skywards. Over the river lies an older Shanghai, including the Bund, the city's waterfront boulevard lined with turn-of-the-century buildings and the intricate maze of the Chinese city. As glamorous address and major tourist attraction, the Grand Hyatt is a symbol of China's economic power: with its 12 restaurants, nightclubs, food courts and bars, including Cloud 9, the Sky Lounge on the 87th floor, seen on facing page, which calls for a dizzy drink on the rooftop of Asia.

Wären Hotels Berge, dann wäre das Grand Hyatt in Shanghai der Mount Everest der Hotelindustrie. Als höchstes Hotel der Welt steht es in der Millenium-Ausgabe des Guinness-Buchs der Rekorde.

Das Hotel verfügt über 555 Zimmer und liegt in den Stockwerken 53 bis 87 (von insgesamt 88) des Jin-Mao-Gebäudes. Die Aussicht über die glitzernde Stadtlandschaft Shanghais ist atemberaubend. Der Fluss Huangpu teilt die Stadt in die Stadtteile Pudong im Osten und Puxi im Westen. Das Grand Hyatt liegt mitten in Pudong, dem Geschäftszentrum der Stadt, dort, wo die Riesentürme in den Himmel ragen. Am anderen Flussufer liegt der ältere Teil Shanghais mit dem Labyrinth der Altstadt und dem Bund, der Uferpromenade, an der zahlreiche Gebäude aus der Jahrhundertwende erhalten blieben. Das Grand Hyatt ist eine glanzvolle Adresse – die bedeutende Touristenattraktion gilt als Symbol der Wirtschaftsmacht China. Das repräsentative Hotel verfügt über zwölf Restaurants, Nachtclubs, Büffettheken und Bars, darunter »Cloud 9« im 87. Stock (linke Seite) in der man einen feinen Drink auf dem Dach Asiens nehmen sollte.

Si les hôtels étaient des montagnes, le Grand Hyatt de Shanghai serait l'Everest de l'industrie hôtelière. Cet hôtel a d'ailleurs fait son entrée dans le livre Guinness des records à l'aube du 21e siècle.

Niché entre les 53e et 87e étages de la Jin Mao Tower, qui en compte 88, cet hôtel de 555 chambres offre une vue imprenable sur les lumières du Shanghai moderne qui s'étale à ses pieds. Le Huangpu partage la ville en deux, entre Pudong à l'est et Puxi à l'ouest. Le Grand Hyatt se trouve au cœur de Pudong, le quartier de la finance dont les tours se lancent à l'assaut des cieux. Il suffit de traverser le fleuve pour se trouver dans le Vieux Shanghai, avec son alignement d'immeubles du tournant du siècle sur le Bund, et le labyrinthe inextricable de la vieille ville. Endroit chic et haut lieu touristique, le Grand Hyatt est un symbole de la puissance économique chinoise: il comprend 12 restaurants, night-clubs, stands de restauration à hème et bars. Siroter une boisson dans le plus impressionnant d'entre eux, le bar panoramique «Cloud 9» situé au 87e étage (page de gauche), sur le toit de l'Asie, est à donner le vertige.

PREVIOUS PAGES Shanghai's shimmering spread on the banks of the Huangpu River viewed from the commanding heights of the Grand Hyatt. FACING PAGE a deluxe room with verse in calligraphy on the headboard. ABOVE view of the city from the Jin Mao Club. BELOW a 180-degree vista of the city from a deluxe room. ✳ VORHERGEHENDE DOPPELSEITE Ausblick aus höchster Höhe vom Grand Hyatt auf Shanghais funkelndes Lichtermeer an den Ufern des Huangpu. LINKE SEITE ein Deluxe-Zimmer mit kalligrafischen Versen auf dem Kopfende des Bettes. OBEN Blick auf die Stadt vom Jin-Mao-Club. UNTEN eine 180-Grad-Aussicht auf die Stadt, aus einem Deluxe-Zimmer. ✳ DOUBLE PAGE PRECEDENTE une vue plongeante sur les lumières de Shanghai qui s'étalent en un tapis lumineux de part et d'autre du Huangpu. PAGE DE GAUCHE Un poème calligraphié orne la tête de lit dans cette chambre de luxe. CI-DESSUS la ville vue du Jin Mao Club. CI-DESSOUS la chambre de luxe offre une vue panoramique sur la ville.

Pia Pierre
SHANGHAI

Cosmopolitan chic
returns to the French Quarter.

Pia Pierre is a French archaeologist who has lived in Asia for nearly 30 years. She began to travel extensively in China in the early 1980s and fell in love with Shanghai's fading cosmopolitan air and hybrid culture.

She dreamed of finding a "pied-a-terre" there but it was not easy. She remembers the British consul facing similar difficulties. "He finally took two rooms at the YMCA, knocked down a wall and created a home." Things changed, Shanghai recovered its worldly outlook, and after much trial and error, she found what she wanted: a house in ruins in the old French concession. "People ran away when they saw it," says Pierre. But the location was pleasant – on a boulevard shaded by plane trees – and there was a discreet garden tucked in the back. Having restored a feudal lord's house in Bangkok and a castle in Provence, she rose to the challenge. Pierre has kept as many of the original features as possible: the marble bathrooms, the Art Deco fireplace and the ironwork veranda grilles. "The place had soul and I tried to respect it."

Die Archäologin Pia Pierre lebt seit fast dreißig Jahren in Asien. Anfang der 1980er Jahre reiste sie ausgiebig durch China und verliebte sich in die hybride Kultur und die schwindende kosmopolitische Atmosphäre Shanghais.

Sie träumte von einem »pied-à-terre«, aber das war schwer zu finden. Pia Pierre erinnert sich daran, dass der britische Konsul vor ähnlichen Problemen stand. »Schließlich nahm er zwei Zimmer im YMCA, machte einen Durchbruch und richtete sich ein.« Shanghai veränderte sich und gab sich erneut einen weltlichen Anstrich, und nach vielen vergeblichen Versuchen fand auch Pia Pierre, was sie suchte: ein verfallenes Haus in der Französischen Konzession. »Beim Anblick des Hauses liefen die Leute reihenweise davon«, erinnert sich die Eigentümerin. Die Lage auf einem Boulevard mit Schatten spendenden Platanen gefiel ihr jedoch, und hinter dem Haus lag ein nicht einsehbarer kleiner Garten. Da sie bereits das Haus eines Feudalherrn in Bangkok und ein Schloss in der Provence restauriert hatte, wagte sich Pierre an die schwierige Aufgabe der Renovierung. Sie erhielt möglichst viele ursprüngliche Elemente wie die Badezimmer aus Marmor, den Kamin im Art-déco-Stil und die schmiedeeisernen Verandagitter. »Ich versuche, die Seele des Hauses zu respektieren.«

Pia Pierre, une archéologue française, vit en Asie depuis une trentaine d'années. Pendant un de ses nombreux voyages en Chine au début des années 1980, elle est tombée amoureuse du cosmopolitisme fané et de la culture métissée de Shanghai.

Elle rêvait d'un pied-à-terre, mais ce n'était pas chose facile. Le consul du Royaume-Uni avait lui aussi connu ce genre de difficultés, raconte-t-elle. Il avait fini par se rabattre sur deux chambres au foyer du YMCA, et avait abattu une cloison pour se créer un chez-soi. Les temps ont changé, Shanghai s'est rouverte au monde et Pia Pierre a fini par trouver ce qu'elle cherchait: une maison en ruine dans l'ancienne concession française. «Son état de délabrement en avait fait fuir plus d'un », confie-t-elle. Mais la maison était bien située, sur un boulevard bordé de platanes dispensant leur ombre, et donnait à l'arrière sur un jardin à l'abri des regards. Pia qui a déjà restauré une demeure féodale à Bangkok et un château en Provence s'est montrée ici à la hauteur de la tâche. Elle a conservé autant d'éléments d'origine que possible: salles de bain en marbre, cheminée Art déco et grilles en fer forgé de la véranda. «Cet endroit avait une âme et j'ai essayé de la respecter.»

FACING PAGE a Ming period calligraphy panel and a Japanese sake jar in the marble entrance hall. **ABOVE** The double-sized living room with its Art Deco-style fireplace is decorated with period furniture and Chinese scrolls. ✳ **LINKE SEITE** eine Kalligrafie-Tafel aus der Ming-Periode und ein japanischer Sakebehälter in der Eingangshalle aus Marmor. **OBEN** Das geräumige Wohnzimmer mit dem Art-déco-Kamin ist mit historischen Möbeln und chinesischen Bildrollen eingerichtet. ✳ **PAGE DE GAUCHE** Un panneau calligraphié de l'ère Ming et une jarre à saké japonaise agrémentent l'entrée en marbre. **CI-DESSUS** Le double living doté d'une cheminée Art déco abrite des meubles d'époque et des rouleaux peints chinois.

FACING PAGE The iron window in the study is original to the house. The elmwood chairs were made for 18th-century officials. ABOVE A canvas by contemporary Chinese artist Liu Wen Quan, whose works are inspired by old engravings, hangs above a black porcelain vase. BELOW A giant metal birdcage and a painting by modern Chinese artist Pang Yang Jie dominate the green living room on the second floor. ✳ LINKE SEITE Das Eisengitterfenster im Arbeitszimmer blieb erhalten. Die Stühle aus Ulmenholz wurden für Beamte aus dem 18. Jahrhundert angefertigt. OBEN Über einer schwarzen Porzellanvase hängt ein Gemälde des zeitgenössischen chinesischen Malers Liu Wen Quan, dessen Werke von alten Stichen inspiriert sind. UNTEN Ein riesiger Vogelkäfig und ein Bild des modernen chinesischen Künstlers Pang Yang Jie beherrschen das in Grün gehaltene Wohnzimmer auf der zweiten Etage. ✳ PAGE DE GAUCHE La fenêtre à châssis métallique du bureau est d'origine. Les chaises en orme ont été fabriquées au 18e siècle pour des mandarins. CI-DESSUS un vase de porcelaine noir sous un tableau peint par l'artiste chinois contemporain Liu Wen Quan, qui s'inspire de gravures anciennes. CI-DESSOUS Une immense cage à oiseaux et un tableau de l'artiste chinois contemporain Pang Yang Jie sont les pièces maîtresses du salon vert, à l'étage.

FUCHUN RESORT
HANGZHOU

In the footsteps of Marco Polo.

"In heaven there is paradise," say the Chinese, "and on earth there is Suzhou and Hangzhou."

»Im Himmel liegt das Paradies«, sagen die Chinesen, »auf Erden Suzhou und Hangzhou«.

«Au ciel, il y a le paradis, sur terre, Suzhou et Hangzhou.» (Dicton chinois)

Hangzhou, in Zhejiang province south of Shanghai, is one of the most celebrated tourist attractions in China, with the freshwater West Lake surrounded by hills, gardens, pavilions and temples; bridges on the Grand Canal and the picturesque course of the Fuchun River. Marco Polo thought so too, when he passed through Hangzhou in the 13th century; as the capital of the Southern Song dynasty, the city became a major producer of fine silks and tea. Hangzhou's scenic splendour was immortalised in a pen-and-ink scroll titled "Living in the Fuchun Mountains" by a master of Yuan dynasty painting in 1347. The Fuchun Resort, a series of elegant villas that stand in terraces of green tea plantation by an 18-hole golf course, convey the spirit in modern times. Planned by architect Jean-Michel Gathy and designer Jaya Ibrahim, the resort is a refined reinterpretation of Song dynasty style.

Die von Hügeln umgebene Stadt Hangzhou in der Provinz Zhejiang südlich von Shanghai ist eines der beliebtesten Touristenziele in China. Sie liegt am Westsee, einem Süßwassersee, und wirkt mit den vielen Gärten, Pavillons und Tempeln, den Brücken über den Kaiserkanal und dem malerischen Lauf des Fuchun-Flusses ausgesprochen pittoresk. Schon Marco Polo war dieser Meinung, als er im 13. Jahrhundert Hangzhou passierte, das sich später als Hauptstadt der südlichen Song-Dynastie zu Seiden- und Teeproduktion in großem Stil aufschwang. Die landschaftliche Schönheit der Stadt wurde von einem Künstler der Yuan-Dynastie bereits 1347 in einer Bleistift-Tusche-Zeichnung mit dem Titel »Das Leben in den Fuchunbergen« verewigt. Der Fuchun Resort, ein Komplex eleganter Villen auf den Terrassen einer Tee-Plantage an einem 18-Loch-Golfplatz, überträgt diesen Geist in unsere modernen Zeiten. Der Resort nach Plänen des Architekten Jean-Michel Gathy und des Designers Jaya Ibrahim stellt eine verfeinerte Interpretation des Stils der Song-Dynastie dar.

Hangzhou, dans la province de Zhejiang, au sud de Shanghai, est un des hauts lieux touristiques de la Chine: on y admire le lac de l'Ouest, un lac d'eau douce entouré de collines, de jardins, de pavillons et de temples, les ponts enjambant le Grand Canal et le cours pittoresque du Fuchun. La ville avait déjà impressionné Marco Polo au 13e siècle. Capitale des Song du Sud, c'était un important centre de production de soieries fines et de thé. La beauté pittoresque de Hangzhou a été immortalisée par un maître de la période Yuan en 1347 dans un rouleau peint à l'encre et au crayon intitulé «La Vie dans les montagnes du Fuchun». Le Fuchun Resort, ensemble d'élégantes villas disséminées dans une plantation de thé en terrasses à proximité d'un golf 18 trous, est empreint de modernité. Fruit de la collaboration entre l'architecte Jean-Michel Gathy et le designer Jaya Ibrahim, le complexe est une réinterprétation toute en finesse du style architectural Song.

PREVIOUS PAGES Each four-bedroom villa has its own heated swimming pool. FACING PAGE The clubhouse lounge serves fine tea, produced in-house on the tea estate. ABOVE Song dynasty sculpture and wood panels decorate the clubhouse lounge. BELOW The entrance to one of the five free-standing villas. FOLLOWING PAGES a view of old bridges on the Grand canal in Hangzhou.
※ VORHERGEHENDE DOPPELSEITE Jede Villa verfügt über vier Schlafzimmer und einen eigenen geheizten Swimmingpool. LINKE SEITE In der Lounge des Clubhauses wird exquisiter Tee serviert, der von der hauseigenen Tee-Plantage stammt. OBEN Eine liegende Statue aus der Zeit der Song-Dynastie ziert die holzvertäfelte Lounge des Clubhauses. UNTEN der Eingang zu einer der fünf frei stehenden Villen. FOLGENDE DOPPELSEITE Blick auf die alten Brücken über dem Kaiserkanal in Hangzhou. ※ DOUBLE PAGE PRECEDENTE Chaque villa possède quatre chambres à coucher et une piscine privée chauffée. PAGE DE GAUCHE Dans le salon du club-house, on peut déguster un thé exquis, produit sur place. CI-DESSUS Une sculpture Song et des panneaux de bois agrémentent le salon du club-house. CI-DESSOUS l'entrée de l'une des cinq villas indépendantes. DOUBLE PAGE SUIVANTE ponts anciens enjambant le Grand canal à Hangzhou.

Yoshifumi Nakamura

Chiiori

The Plastic House

Tenmangu

Isamu Noguchi

Nihon Miyabigoto Club

Japan

Junko Koshino

House of Bamboo

Eizo Shiina

The 4x4 House

The Yagi House

Tenmangu
Near Kyoto

A writer in a 17th-century shrine.

Tenmangu is a shrine dedicated to the patron of scholarship and calligraphy in Japan. There are tens of thousands of Tenmangu shrines across the country. This particular house, in the town of Kameoka to the west of Kyoto, was once the priest's house in the grounds of the Yada-Tenmangu shrine.

Alex Kerr, an American writer, scholar and art dealer who has lived much of his life in Japan, was drawn to it because of his love of calligraphy. It has been his home since 1977. The early 17th-century house was once a nunnery and is in typical Kyoto style: tiled roof, *tatami* floors, sliding *fusuma* doors and wooden drop ceilings. One part of the house, the old kitchen area, is still open to the rafters. In 1984 Alex Kerr remodeled this part into his calligraphy painting and mounting room. But the rest of the house, decorated with Chinese and Japanese rugs, scrolls, classical furniture and folding screens, remains as it was, suffused with a sense of nature and a place of tranquil contemplation and study.

Als Tenmangu bezeichnet man einen Schrein, der dem Schutzpatron der Gelehrsamkeit und Kalligrafie in Japan geweiht ist. Tenmangu-Schreine gibt es zehntausendfach über das ganze Land verstreut. Dieses Haus in der Stadt Kameoka westlich von Kyoto gehörte einst dem Priester, der auf dem Gelände des Yada-Tenmangu-Schreins wohnte.

Es gefiel dem amerikanischen Schriftsteller, Gelehrten und Kunsthändler Alex Kerr, der seit vielen Jahren in Japan lebt und das Haus seit 1977 bewohnt, wegen seiner Liebe zur Kalligrafie. Das aus dem 17. Jahrhundert stammende Haus, das früher Nonnen beherbergte, präsentiert sich im typischen Stil Kyotos: mit Ziegeldach, *tatami*-Böden, *fusuma*-Schiebetüren und Hängedecken aus Holz. Ein Teil des Hauses, der alte Küchenbereich, ist noch immer nach oben offen bis ins Gebälk. 1984 wandelte Alex Kerr ihn in einen Raum um, wo er sich der Kalligrafie und Rahmung widmet. Den Rest des Hauses ließ er in der Dekoration unverändert mit chinesischen und japanischen Teppichen, Schriftrollen, klassischen Möbeln und Schiebe-Trennwänden. So blieb die natürliche Ausstrahlung eines Ortes erhalten, der zu Gelehrsamkeit und stiller Kontemplation einlädt.

Un Tenmangu est un sanctuaire consacré à la divinité protectrice des érudits et des calligraphes. Il existe des dizaines de milliers de temples de ce genre au Japon. Cette maison particulière, dans la ville de Kameoka, à l'ouest de Kyoto, était autrefois la maison du prêtre dans le parc du sanctuaire.

L'Américain Alex Kerr, écrivain érudit et marchand d'art, a passé une grande partie de sa vie au Japon et habite dans cette maison depuis 1977, attiré ici par son amour de la calligraphie. Le bâtiment, un ancien couvent, a été construit au début du 17e siècle dans le style traditionnel de Kyoto : toit couvert de tuiles, sols en *tatamis*, cloisons coulissantes *fusuma* et plafonds bas en bois. Dans l'ancien espace consacré à la cuisine, les poutres sont encore visibles. En 1984, Alex Kerr l'a transformé en atelier où il peut s'adonner à la calligraphie et à l'encadrement. Les autres pièces, décorées avec des tapis chinois et japonais, des rouleaux calligraphiés, des meubles traditionnels et des cloisons à glissière, sont restées en l'état, pénétrées de nature et propices à la contemplation et à l'étude.

※ **FACING PAGES** stone water basin for purification near the shrine. Maple leaves in the Tenmangu shrine garden. **ABOVE** Stepping stones to the house, with view towards the shrine gate and gardens. ※ **LINKE SEITE** Wasserbecken aus Stein zur rituellen Reinigung vor der Annäherung an den Schrein. Ahornblätter im Garten des Tenmangu-Schreins. **OBEN** Steinstufen führen zum Haus, mit Blick auf die Gärten und das Tor zum Schrein. ※ **PAGE DE GAUCHE** Le jardin est jonché de feuilles d'érable et, près du sanctuaire, nous voyons le bassin à ablutions en pierre. **CI-DESSUS** En suivant les pierres on arrive à la maison, et l'on voit la porte du sanctuaire et les jardins en arrière-plan.

※ **PREVIOUS PAGES** The main room overlooks the garden. antique Chinese table holding an incense burner and spirit stone. The traditional floor lamps are known as *andon*. On the floor are early 20th-century *tatami* rugs. **FACING PAGE** Sliding doors of old ink paintings and calligraphy by Alex Kerr link the main room to the bedroom. In the bedroom is a *tatami* bed. Arrangement of lotus pods on a lacquered stand. **ABOVE** A centerpiece of the main room is an impressive calligraphic screen about sacred animals by an Edo-period artist. ※ **VORHER-GEHENDE DOPPELSEITE** Vom größten Zimmer aus überblickt man den Garten. Auf dem antiken chinesischen Tisch stehen ein Räucherstäbchen und ein Geisterstein. Die traditionellen Boden-lampen bezeichnet man als *andon*. **LINKE SEITE** Schiebetüren mit alten Tuschezeichnungen und Kalligrafie von Alex Kerr trennen das große Zimmer vom Schlafzimmer, in dem ein *tatami*-Bett steht. Dekorative Lotushülsen auf einem Lacktablett. **OBEN** Den großen Raum dominiert ein großartiger Wandschirm mit der kalligrafischen Darstellung heiliger Tiere von einem Künstler aus der Edo-Periode. ※ **DOUBLE PAGE PRECEDENTE** Dans la pièce principale qui donne sur le jardin, un brûle-encens et une pierre censée chasser les mauvais esprits animent une table chinoise ancienne. Des lampes traditionelles *andon* sont posées à même le sol recouvert de *tatamis* du début du 20e siècle. **PAGE DE GAUCHE** Des portes coulissantes ornées de motifs anciens à l'encre de Chine et de calligraphies signées Alex Kerr relient la pièce principale à la chambre à coucher avec son lit en tatamis. Des cosses de lotus égaient un plateau en laque. **CI-DESSUS** Un impressionnant paravent montrant des animaux sacrés calligraphiés par un artiste de l'ère Edo domine la pièce principale.

CHiiORi IYA VALLEY
SHiKOKU

A recall of lost Japan.

Chiiori means the "Cottage of the Flute". And there is something magical about the abandoned 18th- century farmhouse that Alex Kerr found in the mysterious mountain gorges of the mist-wrapped Iya Valley on the island of Shikoku.

In his bestselling book "Lost Japan" Alex Kerr movingly describes his infatuation with the untamed landscape of that isolated part of Japan. He bought the dilapidated farmhouse as struggling student in 1973 and laboured for years to restore it, in the process helping to revive the slow, expensive art of rethatching with long-leafed pampas grass. Although divided into four rooms with sliding doors, the lack of walls makes the interior one large space. In the centre are the floor hearths around which the family would cook and keep warm in winters. There is virtually no ceiling. Tobacco was dried in the rafters – huge open beams that give the space a cathedral-like quality. Since 1999, it is home to The Chiiori Project, a movement to preserve Japan's rural environment.

Chiiori bedeutet »Flöten-Häuschen«, und tatsächlich hat das verlassene Bauernhaus aus dem 18. Jahrhundert, das Alex Kerr in den geheimnisvollen Schluchten des nebligen Iya-Tals auf der Insel Shikoku entdeckte, eine zauberhafte Ausstrahlung.

In seinem Bestseller »Lost Japan« beschreibt Alex Kerr auf ergreifende Weise seine Liebe zu der unberührten Landschaft in dieser Region, die von dem restlichen Japan geradezu isoliert erscheint. Er kaufte das baufällige Bauernhaus 1973 und renovierte es jahrelang allein. So trug er auch zur Wiederentdeckung der zeitraubenden teuren Kunst bei, mit deren Hilfe Dächer mit langblättrigem Pampasgras neu gedeckt werden. Es gibt zwar vier, durch Schiebetüren voneinander getrennte Zimmer, aber wegen der fehlenden Wände wirkt das Hausinnere wie ein großer Raum. In der Mitte liegen die Bodenkamine, die früher nicht nur zum Kochen, sondern auch als Wärmequelle im Winter genutzt wurden. In den Dachsparren wurde Tabak getrocknet – mit den breiten Balken wirkt das Haus fast wie eine Kathedrale. Seit 1999 beherbergt es das Chiiori-Projekt, eine Einrichtung, die sich für die Erhaltung der ländlichen Landschaften in Japan einsetzt.

Chiiori signifie «ferme de la flûte». Et il y a comme un enchantement autour de cette ferme du 18ᵉ siècle à l'abandon qu'Alex Kerr a découverte sur l'île de Shikoku, dans les mystérieuses gorges de la vallée d'Iya enveloppée de brume.

Dans son ouvrage «Lost Japan», un succès en librairie, Alex Kerr décrit de manière émouvante son engouement pour les paysages sauvages de cette région reculée du Japon. Il a acheté cette ferme délabrée en 1973, alors qu'il était un étudiant sans le sou, et il a peiné pendant des années pour la restaurer, faisant par la même occasion revivre l'art coûteux et laborieux des toitures en herbe de la pampa. L'espace peut être divisé en quatre pièces au moyen de panneaux coulissants, mais l'absence de cloisons fait de l'intérieur un grand espace. Au centre, se trouve le foyer ouvert servant à la cuisine et autour duquel la maisonnée se réchauffait en hiver. Autrefois, du tabac séchait, suspendu aux chevrons de la charpente apparente qui donne à l'espace une allure de cathédrale. Depuis 1999, la maison abrite le Chiiori Project, association de protection de l'environnement rural japonais.

❋ **FACING PAGE** View of Chiiori with its restored thatched roof. Stockpiles of wood for the long winter. **ABOVE** The farmhouse stands amidst cryptomeria pines and tufts of wild grass. **FOLLOWING PAGES** Alex Kerr found the abandoned farmhouse, with its sweeping views of the valley, in 1973. Old roof tiles were brought from Kyoto for future use in Chiiori. Dense pine trees cover the mountain gorges of Iya Valley. ❋ **LINKE SEITE** Chiiori mit neu gedecktem Strohdach. Holzstapel für den langen Winter. **OBEN** Um das Bauernhaus herum wachsen Sicheltannen und büschelweise Gras. **FOLGENDE DOPPELSEITEN** Alex Kerr entdeckte das Bauernhaus mit der bezaubernden Aussicht auf das Tal im Jahr 1973. Er ließ alte Dachziegel aus Kyoto kommen, um sie in Chiiori wieder zu verwenden. Die Kiefern stehen dicht an dicht in den Bergschluchten des Iya-Tals. ❋ **PAGE DE GAUCHE** Chiiori avec son nouveau toit de chaume. Le bois a été empilé car l'hiver sera long. **CI-DESSUS** La ferme s'élève au milieu des cèdres du Japon et des graminées. **DOUBLES PAGES SUIVANTES** Alex Kerr a découvert en 1973 cette ferme abandonnée qui offre une vue panoramique sur la vallée. Il a fait venir de vieilles tuiles de Kyoto pour les réutiliser à Chiiori. Une épaisse forêt de cèdres recouvre les gorges de la vallée d'Iya.

※ **FACING PAGE** the volunteer staff at Chiiori – Daisuke, Yuki, Ken, Ginevra – with Jackie, the dog. Jackie guards the house. Behind him, three traditional saws are mounted on the wall. **ABOVE** Entrance to the kitchen. A large calligraphic screen by Alex Kerr that he made for a party hangs above a wooden pickle bucket. **FOLLOWING PAGES** A samurai banner with a triple oak leaf crest marks the far wall of the main room. A teapot on a bamboo support hangs over the open hearth. *Andon* lamps and traditional straw mats provide warmth and light. Chiiori staff stoke the traditional hearth in the middle of the room. ※ **LINKE SEITE** Die ehrenamtlichen Mitarbeiter in Chiiori – Daisuke, Yuki, Ken, Ginevra – mit dem Hund Jackie. Jackie bewacht das Haus. Hinter ihm hängen drei traditionelle Sägen an der Hauswand. **OBEN** der Eingang zur Küche. Ein großer kalligrafischer Wandschirm, den Alex Kerr für eine Party anfertigte, hängt über einem Beizeimer aus Holz. **FOLGENDE DOPPELSEITEN** An der hinteren Wand im großen Zimmer hängt ein Samuraibanner mit einem dreifachen Eichenblatt als Wappen. Über dem offenen Kamin hängt ein Teekessel an einer Halterung aus Bambus. *Andon*-Lampen und die traditionellen Strohmatten sorgen für eine warme helle Atmosphäre. Eine Chiiori-Mitarbeiterin schürt in hergebrachter Weise die Feuerstelle mitten im Raum. ※ **PAGE DE GAUCHE** le personnel bénévole de Chiiori – Daisuke, Yuki, Ken, Ginevra – avec le chien Jackie. Jackie monte la garde. Derrière lui, trois scies traditionnelles sont accrochées au mur. **CI-DESSUS** le seuil de la cuisine. Au-dessus d'un baquet à saumure en bois, un grand écran mural calligraphié réalisé par Alex Kerr pour une réception. **DOUBLES PAGES SUIVANTES** Une bannière de samouraï ornée d'un motif à trois feuilles de chêne habille le mur du fond de la pièce principale. Une théière dans son support de bambou est suspendue au-dessus de l'âtre. Des lampes *andon* et des nattes de paille traditionnelles dispensent chaleur et lumière. Une employée entretient le foyer ouvert traditionnel au centre de la pièce.

✻ **ABOVE** stones for grinding *soba* buckwheat noodles with herbs gathered from the hillside. **RIGHT** a round tile-work container for extinguished ashes on a lacquer table before a samurai banner. **FACING PAGE** a lamp by Isamu Noguchi on an old wooden desk. Beyond the door is the kitchen. The calligraphy on the desk reads "Spear". ✻ **OBEN** Mahlsteine für die *soba*-Buchweizennudeln, die mit Kräutern aus den umliegenden Hügeln gewürzt werden. **RECHTS** ein runder Ziegeltopf für erloschene Asche vor einem Samuraibanner. **RECHTE SEITE** eine Isamu-Noguchi-Lampe auf einem alten Schreibtisch aus Holz. Hinter der Tür liegt die Küche. Auf dem Schreibtisch liegt die Kalligrafie das Zeichens »Speer«. ✻ **CI-DESSUS** Des pierres pour moudre la farine de sarrasin des nouilles *soba* qui seront épicées avec les herbes parfumées des collines avoisinantes. **A DROITE** Le récipient rond en terre cuite placé sur une table en laque devant la bannière de samouraï, est destiné à recevoir les cendres éteintes. **PAGE DE DROITE** Une lampe d'Isamu Noguchi sur un bureau en bois ancien. La calligraphie posée sur le bureau signifie « lance ».

Isamu NOGUCHI

MURE SHIKOKU

A sculptor's repose in a stone-cutter's village.

"I am the fusion of two worlds, the East and West," said Isamu Noguchi. "And yet I hope to reflect more than both". The Japanese-American artist, who died in 1988 at the age of 84, was a cult figure in bridging many worlds.

Almost anyone today recognizes his light-as-bubble paper lamps. Noguchi's output was actually prodigious. He worked with some of the great minds of the 20th century: Constantin Brancusi, Buckminster Fuller and Martha Graham, designing stage sets, gardens, public spaces and, above all, sculpture in materials that ranged from terra cotta to stainless steel. But his greatest work was in stone. Rejected by his Japanese father, Noguchi returned again and again to find his roots to try and locate the heart of Japan. In 1970 he found a corner in the stone-cutter's village of Mure (pronounced "moo-ray") on the island of Shikoku. Here he worked, in granite and basalt, learning from stonemasons to distil the abstractions of nature into art. He also restored a samurai farmhouse. Noguchi's home, garden and work space are now a place of pilgrimage.

»Ich verkörpere die Verschmelzung zweier Welten, des Ostens und des Westens«, sagte Isamu Noguchi. »Dennoch hoffe ich, dass meine Kunst mehr ausstrahlt als nur dies.« Der japano-amerikanische Künstler, der 1988 im Alter von 84 Jahren starb, war eine Kultfigur, die viele Kulturen miteinander in Verbindung brachte.

Heute kennt fast jeder seine Papierlampen. Noguchi hat außerordentlich viele Werke geschaffen; er arbeitete mit einigen Geistesgrößen des 20. Jahrhunderts zusammen: Constantin Brancusi, Buckminster Fuller und Martha Graham. Er gestaltete Bühnenbilder, Gärten und öffentliche Räume, und zwar mit verschiedenen Materialien von Terrakotta bis Edelstahl. Seine besten Arbeiten jedoch schuf er aus Stein. Trotz oder wegen der Ablehnung, die Noguchi von seinem japanischen Vater erfuhr, kehrte er auf der Suche nach seinen Wurzeln immer wieder zurück. 1970 fand er sein Eckchen Heimat in dem Steinschneiderdorf Mure (»muh-rei« ausgesprochen) auf der Insel Shikoku. Dort arbeitete er mit Granit und Basalt und lernte von Steinmetzen, das Abstrakte der Natur in Kunst zu verwandeln. Nebenbei restaurierte er ein Samurai-Bauernhaus. Inzwischen pilgern viele Menschen zu Noguchis Haus, seinem Garten und seiner Werkstatt.

« Je suis la fusion de deux mondes, l'Orient et l'Occident », disait Isamu Noguchi. « Et j'espère pourtant refléter plus que la somme des deux. » Cet artiste américano-japonais décédé en 1988 à l'âge de 84 ans, fut une personnalité très admirée qui a su jeter des ponts entre de nombreuses cultures.

Tout le monde ou presque connaît ses lampes en papier de riz qui sculptent la lumière. La production de Noguchi a été véritablement prodigieuse. Il a travaillé avec des grands esprits du 20e siècle, comme Constantin Brancusi, Buckminster Fuller et Martha Graham, créant des décors de scène, des jardins, des espaces publics et, surtout, des sculptures dans une palette de matériaux allant de la terre cuite à l'inox. Mais sa réalisation majeure est de pierre. Rejeté par son père japonais, Noguchi se rendit inlassablement au Japon, à la recherche de ses racines. En 1970, il découvrit un endroit dans le village de tailleurs de pierres de Mure (à prononcer «mou-raï»), sur l'île de Shikoku. Il y travailla le granite et le basalte, apprenant auprès de ces artisans à transformer la nature en art. Il rénova aussi une ancienne ferme de samouraï. Aujourd'hui, la maison de Noguchi, ainsi que son jardin et son espace de travail sont devenus un lieu de pèlerinage.

※ **ABOVE** a study area in Noguchi's house, once a 200-year-old samurai farmhouse. **FACING PAGE** A Noguchi paper lamp lights up the simple interior with its sliging doors and a space with a floor of granite slabs. ※ **OBEN** der Arbeitsbereich in Noguchis Haus, einem 200 Jahre alten Samurai-Bauernhaus. **RECHTE SEITE** Eine von Noguchis berühmten Papierlampen beleuchtet die schlichte Inneneinrichtung mit den Schiebetüren und den mit Granittplatten ausgelegten Nebenraum ※ **CI-DESSUS** Le coin bureau dans la maison de Noguchi, une ferme samouraï vieille de deux siècles. **PAGE DE DROITE** Une lampe en papier Noguchi éclaire cet intérieur sobre doté de cloisons coulissantes et pavé de dalles en granite.

※ **FACING PAGE** A view of the *kura*, the Japanese storehouse, that Noguchi used as his carving studio. the entrance to the compound. **ABOVE** Noguchi's granite sculpture arranged in a sculpture garden. **FOLLOWING PAGES** bamboo and autumn foliage in the back yard. ※ **LINKE SEITE** Blick auf die *kura*, das japanische Lagerhaus, das Noguchi als Bildhauer-Werkstatt nutzte. Der Eingang zum Lager. **OBEN** Noguchis Granitskulpturen in einem Skulpturengarten. **FOLGENDE DOPPELSEITE** Bambus und Herbstlaub im Hinterhof. ※ **PAGE DE GAUCHE** Noguchi a installé son atelier de sculpteur dans une *kura*, un entrepôt japonais. L'entrée du complexe. **CI-DESSUS** le jardin de sculptures en granite réalisées par Noguchi. **DOUBLE PAGE SUIVANTE** bambous et feuillage d'automne dans l'arrière-cour.

NIHON MIYABIGOTO CLUB

TOKYO

Cultivated tradition in a concrete shell.

Rieko Kawabe's calling card is a perfect introduction to her art: made of rich rough-edged handmade paper, it is inscribed with delicate calligraphy in black and rounded off with a faintly-smudged seal in red. Her life's mission is a revival of Japan's traditional arts.

In 1995 Kawabe founded the Nihon Miyabigoto Club in Tokyo to teach calligraphy, tea ceremony, No chanting, music and ceramics. As the club's following grew she needed a permanent space. Today, the surprise of entering a featureless apartment building into the Club's premises is a culture shock. With exactitude and delicacy Kawabe has recreated a classical interior: a series of *tatami* rooms interlinked with sliding *shoji* and *fusuma* doors that end in a narrow pebbled courtyard. A modern kitchen, office and storage for art and tea ceremony materials are artfully hidden behind the screens. The spare, seamless spaces provide an aesthetic backdrop for her students. They are also an ideal show place for each exquisite object, including her artworks.

Rieko Kawabes Visitenkarte verrät viel von ihrer Kunst: Auf der Karte aus schwerem handgeschöpften Papier stehen in Schwarz feine kalligrafische Schriftzeichen, gekrönt von einem roten Siegel. Sie hat sich der Wiederbelebung der traditionellen japanischen Künste verschrieben.

1995 gründete Kawabe den Nihon Miyabigoto Club in Tokio, wo Kalligrafie, die Teezeremonie, No-Gesänge, Musik und Töpfern gelehrt werden. Bald benötigte der Club einen festen Veranstaltungsort. Wer heute die Clubräume in dem unauffälligen Wohnblock betritt, erleidet eine Art Kulturschock. Mit viel Geschmack und Sinn für Details ist Kawabe die Rekonstruktion einer klassischen Inneneinrichtung gelungen. Eine Reihe von *tatami*-Räumen sind durch *shoji*- und *fusuma*-Schiebetüren miteinander verbunden und führen schließlich in einen engen, mit Kieselsteinen ausgelegten Hof. Die moderne Küche, das Arbeitszimmer und ein Abstellraum für Kunstwerke und Utensilien der Teezeremonie sind geschickt hinter Wandschirmen verborgen. Die kargen nahtlos ineinander übergehenden Räume dienen als ästhetischer Hintergrund für die Lehrgänge und eignen sich überdies hervorragend für Ausstellungen ausgewählter Kunstwerke, inklusive ihrer eigenen.

La carte de visite de Rieko Kawabe nous en dit long sur son art: elle est délicatement calligraphiée à l'encre de Chine sur du papier de luxe de fabrication artisanale, avec en touche finale un sceau rouge légèrement appuyé. Toute la vie de l'artiste a tendu vers un seul but: faire revivre les arts traditionnels japonais.

En 1995, elle a fondé à Tokyo le Nihon Miyabigoto Club, consacré à l'enseignement de la calligraphie, de la cérémonie du thé, du No, de la musique et de la céramique. Les membres du club devenant plus nombreux, elle a dû installer ses locaux dans un immeuble banal. Mais celui qui pénètre ici s'expose à un choc culturel, car Kawabe a recréé dans les moindres détails un intérieur traditionnel: une enfilade de pièces à *tatamis* communiquant entre elles par des cloisons coulissantes *shoji* et des portes *fusuma* qui s'ouvrent sur une étroite cour couverte de galets. Elle a habilement dissimulé derrière des paravents une cuisine moderne, un bureau et des rangements pour le matériel destiné aux activités artistiques et à la cérémonie du thé. Cet espace fluide constitue un havre d'esthétisme pour ses élèves et un lieu idéal pour exposer chaque objet délicat, y compris ses œuvres d'art.

※ **PREVIOUS PAGES** the pebbled courtyard of Nihon Miyabigoto Club. The antique apothecary chest contains students' red seals. Green leaves and a sprig of red berries on an Indian stone fragment form an arrangement on a lacquer table. **ABOVE** Sliding *fusuma* doors can divide the long space into several rooms. **FACING PAGE** A lacquer tray with a flower arrangement is placed against a silver and black screen created by Reiko Kawabe. ※ **VORHERGEHENDE DOPPELSEITEN** der mit Kies ausgelegte Hof des Nihon Miyabigoto Club. In dem alten Apothekerschrank wird der rote Siegellack der Studenten aufbewahrt. Grüne Blätter und ein Zweig mit roten Beeren auf einer indischen Scherbe, sorgsam auf einem Lacktisch arrangiert. **OBEN** Mit Hilfe von *fusuma*-Schiebetüren kann der large Raum in mehrere Zimmer unterteilt werden. **RECHTE SEITE** Ein Lacktablett mit einem Blumenarrangement steht vor einem silberschwarzen Wandschirm, den Reiko Kawabe selbst entworfen hat. ※ **DOUBLES PAGES PRECEDENTES** La cour pavée du Nihon Miyabigoto Club. Des sceaux rouges appartenant à des étudiants sont rangés dans ce meuble de pharmacie ancien Des feuilles vertes et une branche de baies rouges sur un fragment de pierre indien sont savamment disposées sur une table en laque. **CI-DESSUS** Les portes à glissière *fusuma* permettent de diviser en plusieurs pièces cet espace tout en longueur. **PAGE DE DROITE** Une composition florale sur plateau en laque se détache sur un paravent argent et noir signé Reiko Kawabe.

ABOVE Rieko Kawabe's collection of old Japanese screens. **RIGHT** A granite tablet inscribed with Japanese lettering and a ceramic bowl against a folding bamboo screen. **FACING PAGE** Ceramic jars hold a profusion of calligraphic brushes. ❊ **OBEN** Rieko Kawabes Sammlung alter japanischer Schriftrollen. **RECHTS** eine Granitplatte mit eingeritzten japanischen Buchstaben und eine Keramikschüssel vor einem klappbaren Wandschirm aus Bambus. **RECHTE SEITE** jede Menge Kalligrafie-Pinsel in Keramikschüsseln. ❊ **CI-DESSUS** Reiko Kawabe est fin collectionneur de rouleaux japonais anciens. **A DROITE** idéogrammes japonais gravés dans une tablette de granite et bol en céramique devant un paravent de bambou pliable. **PAGE DE DROITE** Les récipients en céramique débordent de pinceaux à calligraphie.

TOKYO

A bonsai-sized space for living and learning.

A stove for warmth, a hot bath to lift the spirit, a small garden for nice days and cozy corners to read and write in: that was Yoshifumi Nakamura's brief to himself.

Nakamura is a rare creature in the world of design: a practicing architect, a professor of architecture and an architectural writer. He and his wife Natsumi, a weaver, occupy two top floors of a small building that he designed in a tidy Tokyo suburb. The flat measures 95 spuare metres in all. It conforms to no particular style but is unique for two reasons: ingenious space solutions that include a bridge of wooden panels above a narrow staircase that create a library hideout; and alternating use of light and dark woods – chestnut, oak, pine, teak and the fragrant Japanese cedar called *hinoki* – that give the flow of spaces a distinctive Japanese fluency. Working with traditional artisans, Nakamura designed most of the furniture, the kitchen stove and the *hinoki* hot tub so precious to hold body and soul together in Japan.

Yoshifumi Nakamuras Auftrag an sich selbst lautete: einen Ofen wegen der Wärme, ein heißes Bad zur Aufmunterung, einen kleinen Garten für warme Tage und gemütliche Ecken zum Lesen und Schreiben.

Nakamura arbeitet nicht nur als Architekt, sondern auch als Architekturprofessor und Autor zum Thema. Mit seiner Frau Natsumi, einer Weberin, bewohnt er die beiden obersten Stockwerke eines kleinen Hauses, das er in einem gepflegten Vorort von Tokio bauen ließ. Die Wohnung ist 95 Quadratmeter groß, lässt sich keinem Stil zuordnen und ist aus zwei Gründen bemerkenswert: Raffinierte Raumlösungen enthalten etwa eine Brücke aus Holzplatten über einer engen Treppe, die so eine Leseecke schaffen, sowie die abwechselnde Verwendung heller und dunkler Hölzer. Kastanie, Eiche, Kiefer, Teak und Holz der duftenden japanischen Zeder (*hinoki*) verleihen den ineinander fließenden Räumen eine gewisse japanische Geschmeidigkeit. In Zusammenarbeit mit traditionell arbeitenden Handwerkern entwarf Nakamura die meisten Möbel, den Küchenherd und das *hinoki*-Badebecken, das den Japanern so wichtig ist, weil ein heißes Bad Körper und Seele zusammenhält.

Un poêle pour se réchauffer, un bain chaud pour élever la pensée, un petit jardin pour les beaux jours et des endroits douillets où s'adonner à la lecture et l'écriture, telle était la consigne que Yushifumi Nakamura voulait observer.

Nakamura, architecte en exercice, professeur d'architecture et théoricien de l'architecture, fait figure d'oiseau rare dans sa spécialité. Il occupe avec sa femme Natsumi, tisserande, les deux derniers étages d'un petit immeuble qu'il a conçu dans une banlieue chic de Tokyo. Cet appartement qui fait en tout et pour tout 95 m² ne se conforme à aucun style particulier. Il est unique en son genre pour deux raisons : des idées ingénieuses sur le plan du traitement de l'espace, notamment une passerelle en bois au-dessus d'une cage d'escalier étroite qui tient lieu de bibliothèque escamotable ; et l'emploi alterné d'essences de bois claires et foncées – noyer, chêne, pin, teck et hinoki, une variété japonaise de cèdre dégageant un parfum agréable – qui donnent à l'espace une fluidité toute nipponne. C'est en collaborant avec des artisans traditionnels que Nakamura a dessiné la plupart des meubles, le poêle de la cuisine et le baquet en bois d'*hinoki* où l'on prend des bains chauds, si importants au Japon pour l'harmonie du corps et de l'esprit.

The celadon glow of plastic.

It is a truth universally acknowledged that a young man in love will soon need a house. And so it was that when Tokyo-based fashion photographer Rowland Kirishima – handsome, clever and of mixed Japanese-American parentage – met his future wife Noriko through a grand master of the tea ceremony he wanted a proper home.

Kirishima's original idea was to find a loft that would combine a living area and photo studio. Instead, he found a narrow suburban plot and wanted the famous Kengo Kuma to design a house. Deeply impressed by Kuma's bamboo architecture, he took courage in both hands and approached him. Kuma was enthusiastic. Bamboo was rejected for plastic, as a symbol of Tokyo's "newness and change". But what kind of plastic? One choice was to create a Lego-like structure of phenol plastic without a steel frame. But the government banned the use of phenol as a building material. So Kuma built the house entirely from polycarbonate panels, a material used for bathtubs. At night the house glows like a translucent jade jewel.

Jeder weiß, dass ein verliebter junger Mann bald ein Haus braucht. So auch der Modefotograf Rowland Kirishima aus Tokio, der – gutaussehend, klug und japano-amerikanischer Herkunft – seine zukünftige Frau Noriko durch einen Großmeister der Teezeremonie kennen lernte.

Er brauchte ein Haus und suchte zunächst nach einem Loft, in dem er Wohnbereich und Fotostudio vereinbaren könnte. Stattdessen fand er ein kleines Grundstück in einem Vorort und träumte davon, Kengo Kuma als Architekten zu gewinnen. Kirishima war begeistert von Kumas Bambusarchitektur und fragte den berühmten Mann. Kuma akzeptierte den Auftrag, verwarf aber Bambus als Material zu Gunsten von Kunststoff als Symbol für Frische und Wandel Tokios. Aber welche Art Kunststoff? Erst wurde angedacht, eine Lego-artige Struktur aus Phenoplasten ohne Stahlrahmen zu bauen, aber Phenol war als Baumaterial gesetzlich verboten. Schließlich baute Kuma das ganze Haus aus Polykarbonatplatten – einem Material, das sonst für Badewannen benutzt wird. Nachts leuchtet das Haus wie ein durchsichtiger Jadestein.

C'est une vérité universelle: un jeune homme amoureux a rapidement besoin d'une maison. Et lorsque le photographe de mode établi à Tokyo Rowland Kirishima – un Américano-japonais, beau et intelligent – a rencontré Noriko, sa future femme, par l'intermédiaire d'un grand maître de la cérémonie du thé, lui aussi a voulu une maison à lui.

Au départ, Kirishima rêvait d'un loft qui abriterait une partie habitation et un studio photo. A la place, il a trouvé un terrain en banlieue et, très impressionné par l'architecture de bambou de Kengo Kuma, il a décidé que le célèbre architecte y construirait une maison. Prenant son courage à deux mains, il l'a entrepris sur la question. Le projet a enchanté Kuma qui a cependant délaissé le bambou au profit du plastique, symbole de la «nouveauté et du changement» de Tokyo. Mais quel plastique choisir? Un des concepts prévoyait une structure à partir de modules en phénols sans ossature métallique. Seul problème: l'emploi de phénols dans le bâtiment est interdit au Japon. C'est pourquoi Kuma a construit la maison entièrement en panneaux de polycarbonate, matériau utilisé pour les baignoires. La nuit, la maison chatoie comme un bijou de jade transparent.

❋ **PREVIOUS PAGES** Noriko Kirishima with her baby daughter Kyra. The staircase treads are made of the same polycarbonate panels as much of the house. **ABOVE** At night the tiny three-storied plastic house glows like a jewel in a row of suburban houses. **RIGHT** Exterior air conditioning units were put on the roof and covered with plastic panels. **FACING PAGE** The second floor balcony of the house is framed to encompass a view of a public park across the street. ❋ **VORHERGEHENDE DOPPELSEITE** Noriko Kirishima mit Baby Kyra. Wie fast alles im Haus sind auch die Treppenstufen aus Polykarbonatplatten gefertigt. **OBEN** Nachts leuchtet das kleine dreistöckige Haus wie ein Juwel unter den anderen Häusern im Vorort. **RECHTS** Die Klimaanlage wurde aufs Dach verlegt und mit Kunststoffplatten umbaut. **RECHTE SEITE** Der Balkon auf der zweiten Etage ist seitlich eingerahmt, um den Blick auf den öffentlichen Park auf der anderen Straßenseite zu fokussieren. ❋ **DOUBLE PAGE PRECEDENTE** Noriko Kirishima avec leur fille Kyra. Les marches de l'escalier sont en panneaux de polycarbonate, comme beaucoup de choses dans la maison. **CI-DESSUS** La nuit, la minuscule maison de plastique sur trois niveaux chatoie comme un bijou dans une rangée de maisons de banlieue. **A DROITE** La climatisation a été reléguée sur le toit et recouverte de panneaux de plastique. **PAGE DE DROITE** Le balcon du deuxième étage a été conçu pour que l'on puisse embrasser du regard un jardin public sur le trottoir d'en face.

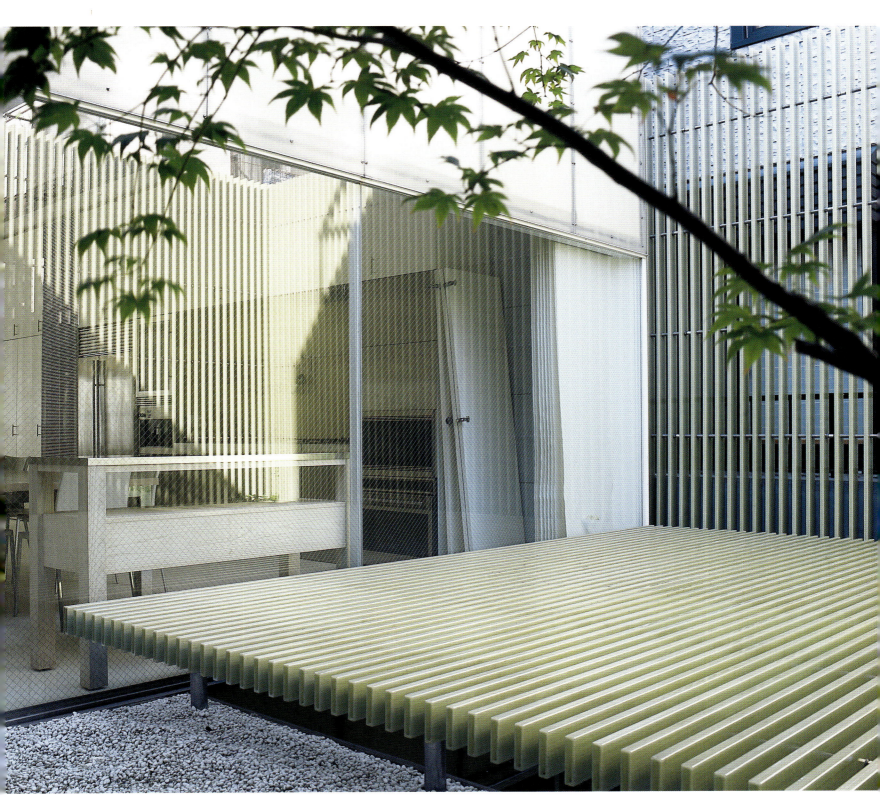

✳ **FACING PAGE** Despite the use of film on windows to block light, the shadows created are as in traditional *shoji* doors. A diffused light filters in through the walls to create a constant play of shadows. **ABOVE** The raised, slatted platform in the rear garden is used for performing tea ceremony. It also lets in light to the basement below. **FOLLOWING PAGES** To increase the illusion of space, the architect gave the living area no windows. The basement bathroom opens on to a dry area to allow natural light. The spare furnishings and monochromatic colour scheme harks back to the tradition of Edo-period houses. ✳ **LINKE SEITE** Obwohl die Fenster mit einer Licht abweisenden Schicht bezogen sind, wirken die Schatten wie bei den traditionellen *shoji*-Schiebetüren. Durch die Wände dringt diffuses Licht. So entstehen ständig wechselnde Schattenspiele. **OBEN** Auf der erhöhten Latten-Plattform im Garten wird die Tee-Zeremonie zelebriert. Außerdem fällt durch die Zwischenräume Licht in den darunter liegenden Keller. **FOLGENDE DOPPELSEITEN** Der Architekt hat für das Wohnzimmer keine Fenster vorgesehen, um die Illusion eines größeren Raumes zu erhalten. An das Bad im Keller schließt sich ein Trockenraum mit natürlichem Licht an. Die karge einfarbige Einrichtung bezieht sich auf die Tradition der Edo-Periode. ✳ **PAGE DE GAUCHE** Malgré le film pare-soleil sur les fenêtres, des ombres courent, comme sur les portes traditionnelles *shoji*. Une lumière diffuse traverse les parois et crée un jeu d'ombre constant. **CI-DESSUS** La cérémonie du thé est célébrée sur l'estrade en caillebotis dans le jardin de derrière ; elle assure aussi l'éclairage naturel du sous-sol. **DOUBLES PAGES SUIVANTES** Afin de renforcer l'illusion d'espace, l'architecte n'a prévu aucune fenêtre dans le séjour. La salle de bains en sous-sol est naturellement éclairée. Le mobilier dépouillé et la monochromie renouent avec la tradition de l'ère Edo en matière d'habitat.

JUNKO KOSHINO

TOKYO

A private view of Tokyo Tower and Mount Fuji.

Junko Koshino is sometimes described as the Vivienne Westwood or Diane von Furstenberg of Japan. Neither comparison is altogether apt. She is a tiny figure, a person of few words and a deeply committed wife and mother, who has built one of the best-known Japanese fashion labels from scratch.

Her eyrie on top of a famous building in the heart of Tokyo – with commanding views of Roppongi Hills and Tokyo Tower on one side and of Mount Fuji on the other – is a homage to contemporary minimalist chic, in a country that has generously contributed to concepts of minimalism. Koshino says her interior was inspired by the theme of a lighthouse, and she wanted to live in a potent conjunction of "urban tension and dramatic beauty, both natural and man-made." Her vast open-plan apartment is a narrative of modern and traditional elements that encompass water and sky, stone and wood, tea ceremony room and entertainment space around an open air atrium. "When Sir Norman Forster came", says Koshino, "he stood transfixed in one corner for 30 minutes."

Manche sehen in Junko Koshino die Antwort Japans auf Vivienne Westwood oder Diane von Fürstenberg – beide Vergleiche treffen jedoch nicht den Punkt. Sie ist klein, macht wenig Worte und hat aus dem Nichts eine der bekanntesten japanischen Modemarken aufgebaut.

Ihr Adlerhorst auf der Spitze eines der berühmtesten Gebäude mitten in Tokio – mit umwerfender Aussicht auf die Roppongi-Hügel und den Tokyo Tower auf der einen sowie auf den Berg Fuji auf der anderen Seite – ist eine Hommage an den zeitgenössischen Minimalismus. Koshino zufolge dachte sie bei ihrem Entwurf der Inneneinrichtung an einen Leuchtturm. Außerdem wollte sie in einer mächtigen Verbindung von »städtischer Spannung und dramatischer Schönheit, die sowohl natürlich als auch künstlich erzeugt sind«, leben. Ihre weitläufige Großraumwohnung beinhaltet moderne und traditionelle Elemente: Wasser und Himmel spielen eine große Rolle, auch Stein und Holz. Es gibt einen Raum für die Teezeremonie und ein Open-Air-Atrium. »Als Sir Norman Forster hier war«, sagt Koshino, »stand er eine halbe Stunde lang stumm in einer Ecke.«

On dit parfois de Junko Koshino qu'elle est la Vivienne Westwood ou la Diane von Fürstenberg du Japon. Ces comparaisons ne sont pas tout à fait appropriées. C'est une femme de petite taille, taciturne, une épouse et mère dévouée, qui a mis sur pied à partir de rien l'une des marques de prêt-à-porter japonaises les plus connues.

Son nid d'aigle au faîte d'un immeuble célèbre du centre de Tokyo – avec une vue spectaculaire sur les collines de Roppongi et la Tokyo Tower d'un côté et le mont Fuji de l'autre – est un hommage au chic minimaliste contemporain, dans un pays qui a largement contribué à la formation de la pensée minimaliste. Koshino affirme avoir puisé l'inspiration pour son intérieur dans le thème du phare et dit qu'elle voulait vivre dans une conjonction forte de «tension urbaine et de beauté dramatique, à la fois naturelle et produit de la main de l'homme». Son vaste appartement marie les éléments modernes et les éléments traditionnels, l'eau et le ciel, la pierre et le bois ; il abrite une pièce réservée à la cérémonie du thé et un espace de détente autour d'un atrium à ciel ouvert. «Le jour où Sir Norman Foster y est venu, confie la créatrice, il est resté pétrifié dans un coin pendant une demi-heure.»

✻ **FACING PAGE** Bars of light reflect on the black slate water body in the open-air atrium. A small bamboo garden is visible through steps to an upper floor. **ABOVE** the living room with its views of central Tokyo. **FOLLOWING PAGES** Sliding doors to kitchen cabinets reveal a wealth of antique lacquer and china. ✻ **LINKE SEITE** An allen Seiten führen Schiebetüren aus Tafelglas in das zentral gelegene Atrium mit dem Wasserbecken. Durch die aufwärts führenden Stufen blickt man in einen Bambusgarten. **OBEN** Das Wohnzimmer mit Ausblick auf das Zentrum von Tokio. Lichtstreifen reflektieren auf dem schieferschwarzen Wasser im Open-Air-Atrium. **FOLGENDE DOPPELSEITE** Die Schiebetüren der Küchenschränke geben den Blick frei auf wahre Schätze von antikem Lack- und Porzellangeschirr. ✻ **PAGE DE GAUCHE** L'atrium central doté d'un bassin est entouré de portes vitrées coulissantes. En regardant entre les marches de l'escalier qui mène au niveau supérieur on aperçoit un petit jardin de bambous. **CI-DESSUS** Les vastes baies du séjour donnent sur le centre de Tokyo. Dans l'atrium, des rais de lumière se reflètent sur l'eau noire comme de l'ardoise. **DOUBLE PAGE SUIVANTE** Derrière des portes à glissières, les placards de cuisine et leurs trésors de vaisselle ancienne en laque et en porcelaine.

EIZO SHiiNA TOKYO

Stargazing through the bamboo curtain.

Architect Eizo Shiina and his house have much in common: they are both small, precise and lit by flashes of fantasy and humor.

Passing through mile after mile of Tokyo's dreary suburbs, one fetches up outside a concrete gate leading to a bamboo grove. Peeping from the treetops is a dome: it is Shiina's private astronomical observatory. One of the architect's favorite sayings centers on star-gazing: "The concept of area belongs to the measurable world. But the concept of space belongs to the unmeasured world." Shiina designed the two-storied house for his sister and himself. His apartment on the first floor, excluding a tiny bedroom, is a large concrete space with a wooden floor. The centrepiece is a fireplace that Shiina calls the "guardian deity" of the house. A bathroom with glass doors and circular vents is designed as an inner garden. The picture window gives on to a minuscule triangular balcony to seat two people. The sound of wind rustling in the maples and bamboo transports you to another world.

Der Architekt Eizo Shiina hat mit seinem Haus viel gemeinsam: Beide sind klein, präzise veranlagt und mit Fantasie und Humor gesegnet.

Nach einer endlosen Fahrt durch die trostlosen Vororte Tokios landet man vor einem Betontor, das in einen Bambushain führt. Über den Baumspitzen erkennt man eine Kuppel: Shiinas privates Observatorium. Einer der beliebtesten Sprüche des Architekten zum Thema Sterngucker lautet: »Der Begriff Fläche gehört in die messbare Welt. Der Begriff (Welt-)Raum jedoch gehört in die unermessene Welt.« Shiina entwarf das zweistöckige Gebäude für sich und seine Schwester. Seine Wohnung im ersten Stock besteht neben einem Schlafzimmer aus einem großen Betonraum mit Holzfußboden. Das Herzstück ist eine Feuerstelle, die Shiina als »Schutzgöttin« des Hauses bezeichnet. Ein Badezimmer ist mit den Glastüren und runden Lüftungsschächten wie ein innerer Garten angelegt. Das Aussichtsfenster führt auf einen winzigen dreieckigen Balkon mit nur zwei Sitzplätzen hinaus. Das Rauschen des Windes in den Ahornbäumen und Bambusstauden versetzt jeden in eine andere Welt.

L'architecte Eizo Shiina et sa maison ont de nombreux points communs: la petite taille, la précision ainsi que la fantaisie et l'humour fulgurants.

Après avoir traversé des kilomètres et des kilomètres de mornes banlieues tokyoïtes, on finit par arriver devant un portail de béton menant à une bambouseraie. Entre les cimes des arbres se profile un dôme, l'observatoire privé de Shiina, qui se plaît à citer un dicton relevant de l'astronomie: «La notion de surface appartient au monde mesurable, tandis que la notion d'espace appartient au monde non mesuré.» Shiina a imaginé cette maison à deux niveaux pour sa sœur et lui-même. Son appartement situé au premier étage est, exception faite d'une minuscule chambre à coucher, un vaste espace de béton avec parquet. Une cheminée, que Shiina appelle la «divinité protectrice» de la maison, occupe une place centrale dans la maison. Dotée de portes vitrées et de puits d'aération circulaires, la salle de bains a été conçue comme une cour intérieure. La fenêtre panoramique donne sur un minuscule balcon triangulaire fait pour deux personnes. Le bruissement du vent dans les érables et les bambous vous transporte dans un autre monde.

※ **ABOVE** The concrete entrance at ground level leads to a thickly planted bamboo grove. **RIGHT** A triangular window echoes the triangular balcony draped with branches of maple. **FACING PAGE** straw slippers on the window sill for stepping onto the balcony. ※ **OBEN** Der ebenerdige Beton-Eingang führt in einen dichten Bambushain. **RECHTS** Das dreieckige Fenster wirkt wie ein Echo auf den dreieckigen, mit Ahornblättern umrankten Balkon. **RECHTE SEITE** Auf dem Fensterbrett liegen Strohsandalen zum Betreten des Balkons. ※ **CI-DESSUS** L'entrée en béton du rez-de-chaussée mène à une bambouseraie très dense. **A_DROITE** Une fenêtre triangulaire fait écho au balcon en triangle décoré de branches d'érable. **PAGE DE DROITE** sur le rebord de la fenêtre, des tongs en paille pour se déplacer sur le balcon.

1983
SELFCONSCIOUS NATURE

※ **FACING PAGE** The central fireplace, the "guardian deity" of the house, is flanked by two counters: one is the kitchen and the other a study. The kitchen stove has a hood of concrete. Recessed spaces in the concrete wall become storage areas. **ABOVE** The main room's concrete walls and ceiling lead to the garden-like bathroom. The large picture window opens onto the balcony. ※ **LINKE SEITE** Die zentrale Feuerstelle, die »Schutzgöttin« des Hauses, grenzt auf der einen Seite an die Küche, auf der anderen an einen Schreibtisch. Über dem Herd hängt ein Abzug aus Beton. Die Nischen in der Betonwand bieten willkommene Abstellflächen. **OBEN** Die Betonwände und die Betondecke des Hauptraums gehen in das als gartenartig konzipierte Badezimmer. Hinter dem großen Aussichtsfenster liegt der Balkon. ※ **PAGE DE GAUCHE** La cheminée centrale, « divinité protectrice » de la maison, est flanquée d'une cuisine et, de l'autre côté, d'un bureau. La hotte de cheminée en béton ; les niches aménagées dans le mur de béton servent de rangements. **CI-DESSUS** Dans le prolongement des murs et du plafond en béton, une salle de bains aux airs de jardin. La grande fenêtre panoramique donne sur le balcon.

HOUSE OF BAMBOO

Kamakura

Medieval Japan enshrined in a modern mystery.

"Number 54…The house with the bamboo door…bamboo roof and bamboo walls…They've even got a bamboo floor…House of Bamboo!" So ran a popular hit of the 1960s. But Rieko Kawabe's bamboo house, in the historic seaside town of Kamakura about an hour's drive south of Tokyo, is nothing like the swingers' shack described in the old song.

Its air of Zen-like serenity and restraint derives from tenets laid down by medieval poets and Buddhist scholars for the building of temples and hermitages. Kawabe also had sentimental reasons for building the bamboo house: she went to school in Kamakura and the property on the bay belonged to her father. 118 varieties of bamboo are grown in Japan. Working with skilled artisans from Kyoto and using particular kinds of bamboo for screens and floors, she has reinvented tradition to create a meditative retreat – and a welcome escape from the cramped spaces of Tokyo. Yoritomo Minamoto, the great samurai and shogun who ruled Kamakura in the 12th century, would have approved.

»Nummer 54 … das Haus mit der Bambustür … Bambusdach und Bambuswände … sogar der Boden ist aus Bambus … ein Bambushaus!« Dieser Song war in den 1960er Jahren ein Hit. Doch Rieko Kawabes Bambushaus in dem alten Seebad Kamakura, eine Autostunde südlich von Tokio, ist alles andere als eine Hippiehütte.

Die heitere und zurückgenommene Zen-Atmosphäre geht auf die Lehrsätze mittelalterlicher Dichter und buddhistischer Gelehrter zum Bau von Tempeln und Klausen zurück. Auch aus sentimentalen Gründen baute Kawabe das Bambushaus: Sie ist in Kamakura zur Schule gegangen, und das Grundstück an der Bucht gehörte ihrem Vater. In Japan wachsen 118 Bambusarten. Indem Kawabe geschickte Handwerker aus Kyoto beauftragte und bestimmte Bambusarten für die Herstellung der Wandschirme und Böden wählte, schuf sie eine traditionelle mittelalterlich anmutende Zufluchtsstätte vor dem ewigen Platzmangel in Tokio. Yoritomo Minamoto, der berühmte Samurai und Shogun, der Kamakura im 12. Jahrhundert regierte, hätte applaudiert.

« Le n° 54 … La maison à la porte en bambou … au toit et aux murs de bambou … Ils ont même un sol en bambou … La maison de bambou! » C'étaient les paroles d'un tube des années 1960, mais la maison de bambou de Rieko Kawabe, située dans la ville balnéaire historique de Kamakura, à environ une heure de voiture au sud de Tokyo, n'a rien à voir avec la cabane décrite dans cette vieille chanson.

Elle doit son ambiance, toute de sérénité zen et de mesure, aux préceptes fixés par des poètes du Moyen Age et des érudits bouddhistes en matière de construction de temples et d'ermitages. Kawabe a aussi choisi une maison de bambou pour des raisons sentimentales : elle a été à l'école à Kamakura et la parcelle sur la baie appartenait à son père. On cultive au Japon 118 variétés de bambou. Avec le concours d'artisans qualifiés de Kyoto et en recourant à des bambous de nature particulière pour les paravents et les sols, elle a réinventé la tradition pour créer un lieu de retraite qui invite à la méditation et permet d'échapper aux espaces exigus de la capitale. Yoritomo Minamoto, célèbre samouraï et shogun qui régna sur Kamakura au 12e siècle, aurait approuvé.

※ **FACING PAGE** The elevation of the two-storeyed bamboo house is layered by multiple bamboo screens of varying heights. The double-height bamboo screens extend to the terrace. **ABOVE** Sliding doors are lined with bamboo. A bamboo roof and bamboo floor create a work space of Zen-like austerity. **FOLLOWING PAGES** A terrace composed of bamboo frames the sea view. In the living room, old inscribed bamboo sticks are used as decorative panels. A bamboo partition screens a storage area. A bamboo spout in the bathroom. ※ **LINKE SEITE** Die Fassade des zweistöckigen Hauses ist von verschiedenen Schichten unterschiedlich hoher Bambuswände geprägt. Die Bambuswände erstrecken sich über zwei Stockwerke bis zur Terrasse. **OBEN** Die Schiebetüren sind mit Bambus verkleidet. Das Bambusdach und der Bambusboden bewirken eine Zen-artige Nüchternheit. **FOLGENDE DOPPELSEITEN** Die Bambusterrasse geht aufs offene Meer hinaus. Ein Stück Treibholz und ein Steinkreis verweisen auf den entfernten Horizont. Im Wohnzimmer werden alte beschriftete Bambusstangen zur Dekoration verwendet. Ein Raumteiler aus Bambus verstellt den Blick auf eine Abstellkammer. Ein Bambusrohr im Badezimmer. ※ **PAGE DE GAUCHE** Des pare-soleil en bambou de différentes hauteurs se surimposent à la façade de la maison à deux niveaux. Les écrans en bambou s'élèvent sur deux niveaux jusqu'à la terrasse. **CI-DESSUS** Le bambou est omniprésent sur les portes coulissantes, le plafond et le sol, conférant à de cet espace de travail une touche d'austérité zen. **DOUBLES PAGES SUIVANTES** La terrasse donne sur la mer. Des tiges de bambou gravées anciennes décorent le salon. Une cloison de bambou dissimule des rangements. Un tuyau en bambou dans la salle de bains.

※ **ABOVE** Rieko Kawabe creates an arrangement of dried autumn leaves with green bamboo. **FACING PAGE** Bamboo pillars and wild grass form a natural backdrop for an outdoor table setting. ※ **OBEN** Rieko Kawabe arrangiert Herbstlaub mit grünem Bambus. **RECHTE SEITE** Bambussäulen und wildes Gras bieten die ideale natürliche Umgebung für eine Sitzgelegenheit unter freiem Himmel. ※ **CI-DESSUS** Rieko Kawabe arrange avec art des feuilles d'automne et des bambous verts. **PAGE DE DROITE** Des colonnes de bambou et des graminées créent un décor idéal pour la salle à manger en plein air.

THE YAGI HOUSE
OSAKA

Tadao Ando, exemplar of Japanese modernism at its most challenging, is fascinated by the problem of building in a destructible landscape. Osaka, where he is based, suffered a major earthquake in 1997 in which hundreds of people perished or were injured.

It was a tragedy that affected Ando deeply. Ryozo Yagi and his family survived the earthquake but their family home was razed to the ground. It had stood on a hillside slope in the prosperous suburb of Shukugawa. Ando built a new house for the Yagi family, more than one structure in concrete, steel and glass. Created around a sunken courtyard and terraced gardens that Ando helped to landscape and plant, the Yagi house has a feeling of solidity and lightness. Ando also designed much of the furniture in the house that the Yagis share with their two grown-up children. Two of its exciting features are a narrow dining room that captures a view of mountains across the valley and Ando's take on the traditional *tatami* room for the tea ceremony.

Tadao Ando, die Lichtgestalt des japanischen Modernismus, ist fasziniert von der problematischen Aufgabe, ein Haus in einer von Erdbeben bedrohten Gegend zu bauen. Er lebt in Osaka, wo 1997 hunderte von Menschen bei einem Erdbeben getötet oder verletzt wurden.

Ryozo Yagi und seine Familie haben die Tragödie, die Ando sehr getroffen hat, überlebt, aber ihr Haus war bis auf die Grundmauern zerstört. Es hatte auf einem Hügel am Hang in dem wohlhabenden Vorort Shukugawa gestanden. Ando baute der Familie Yagi ein neues Haus, das mehr darstellt als ein Gebäude aus Stahl, Beton und Glas. Das Yagi-Haus, das um einen abgesenkten Hof und Terrassengärten herumgebaut wurde, die Ando ebenfalls entworfen hat, strahlt Stabilität und Leichtigkeit zugleich aus. Auch am Entwurf der Inneneinrichtung des Hauses, das die Yagis mit ihren beiden erwachsenen Kindern bewohnen, war Ando beteiligt. Besonders faszinierend sind das schmale Esszimmer mit Blick auf die umliegenden Berge sowie Andos Version des traditionellen *tatami*-Zimmers für die Teezeremonie.

Tadao Ando, qui représente le modernisme japonais dans ce qu'il a de plus provocateur, est fasciné par les problèmes de la construction antisismique. Osaka, où il est installé, a subi en 1997 un séisme grave qui a fait des centaines de morts et de blessés.

Cette tragédie l'a profondément affecté. Si Ryozo Yagi et sa famille ont survécu au tremblement de terre, il n'est resté de leur maison qu'un tas de ruines. Au même emplacement, à flanc de coteau dans la banlieue favorisée de Shukugawa, Tadao Ando a construit pour le couple et ses deux enfants majeurs plus qu'une structure en béton, acier et verre. Organisée autour d'une cour intérieure et de jardins en terrasses à la conception et à la réalisation desquels il a participé, la maison donne une impression de solidité et de légèreté. L'architecte a aussi conçu une grande partie du mobilier. A noter, une salle à manger étroite d'où l'on embrasse du regard les montagnes de l'autre côté de la vallée, et l'emprunt au thème traditionnel de la pièce au sol recouvert de *tatamis* pour la cérémonie du thé.

※ **FACING PAGE** A square window in a wall links the pools of greenery. The hot water tub is of traditional cedar. **ABOVE** The upper garden looks into the sunken courtyard. **FOLLOWING PAGES** The natural shaped stone is used as a water basin in the courtyard. ※ **LINKE SEITE OBEN** Ein viereckiges Fenster in der Mauer verbindet die grünen Inseln. Das Badebecken ist traditionell aus Zedernholz. **OBEN** Der Garten liegt über dem abgesenkten Innenhof. **FOLGENDE DOPPELSEITE** Der von der Natur so geformte Stein wird im Hof als Wasserbecken benutzt. ※ **PAGE DE GAUCHE** Une ouverture carrée ménagée dans un mur fait le lien entre les îlots de verdure. Le baquet est en cèdre, matériau traditionnel. **CI-DESSUS** Le jardin est situé au-dessus de la cour intérieure. **DOUBLE PAGE SUIVANTE** Dans la cour, une pierre aux formes naturelles sert de bassin.

※ **FACING PAGE** The long narrow dining room with its oak fittings overlooks an impressive view of the hills across the town. The oak floor staircase and furniture were designed to Ando's specifications. **ABOVE** a pair of armchairs in a quiet corner of the house. **FOLLOWING PAGES** Ando designed a *tatami* room for the tea ceremony of grey-painted plasterboard that conceals a *shoji* screen and modern *tokonoma*. ※ **LINKE SEITE** Das lange schmale in Eiche gehaltene Esszimmer bietet eine atemberaubende Sicht auf die umliegenden Berge. Die Treppe aus Eichenholz und die Möbel wurden nach Andos Entwürfen angefertigt. **OBEN** zwei Sessel in einer stillen Ecke des Hauses. **FOLGENDE DOPPELSEITE** Der von Ando entworfene *tatami*-Raum für die Teezeremonie besteht aus grün gestrichenem Gipskarton. Dahinter sind ein *shoji*-Wandschirm und eine moderne *tokonoma* verborgen. ※ **PAGE DE GAUCHE** L'étroite salle à manger où domine le chêne offre une vue spectaculaire sur les collines avoisinantes. L'escalier et le mobilier en cèdre ont été fabriqués d'après les dessins de l'architecte. **CI-DESSUS** Deux fauteuils dans un endroit calme de la maison. **DOUBLE PAGE SUIVANTE** Dans la pièce au sol recouvert de tatamis créée par Tadao Ando pour la cérémonie du thé, un panneau en placoplâtre dissimule une cloison *shoji* et un *tokonoma* moderne.

THC
4x4
HOUSE
KOBE

Wrapped in the mists of the Inland Sea.

Is it a modern lighthouse or a magic tower? An innocent exercise with building blocks or a totem-like homage to Japan's mysterious Inland Sea?

With breathtaking views of the Akashi suspension bridge linking Kobe city to Awaji island, the 4 x 4 house – so called because the four-storey tower has a floor plan of exactly four square metres – is a miniature masterpiece by Tadao Ando. It was built for Yoshinari Nakata, an architect and property developer, who bought a 300 square metres beachfront plot for sentimental reasons: he was born and raised on Awaji island. Ando's top-most cube juts out and is off-center by one meter: this is to create space for a staircase. The ground floor accommodates the foyer and bathroom; the bedroom is on the first floor; the study is located on the second; and the living room and kitchen on the fourth. Nakata finds living in the tower a de-stressing exercise. His anxiety levels dip as he falls in with the rhythmic movements of the sun and sea. "I want to live here forever even if my legs give up."

Ist das ein Leuchtturm oder ein verzaubertes Hochhaus? Unschuldige Spielerei mit Bauklötzen oder eine totemähnliche Hommage an Japans geheimnisvolle Inlandsee?

Das 4 x 4-Haus heißt so, weil es aus vier Stockwerken mit einer Grundfläche von jeweils vier Quadratmetern besteht, und ist mit seinem atemberaubenden Ausblick auf die Akashi-Hängebrücke (die Kobe mit der Insel Awaji verbindet) ein herausragendes Meisterwerk in miniature. Tadao Ando baute es für den Architekten und Makler Yoshinari Nakata, der das 300 Quadratmeter große Grundstück am Strand aus Nostalgie gekauft hat, denn er stammt von der Insel Ajawi. Andos oberster Würfel steht asymmetrisch einen Meter vor, damit auch die Treppe Platz hat. Im Erdgeschoss befinden sich Eingang und Badezimmer, das Schlafzimmer liegt im ersten Stock, das Arbeitszimmer im zweiten und Wohnzimmer und Küche liegen im dritten Stock. Nakata empfindet das Leben im Turm als eine Entspannungsübung. Im Rhythmus von Sonne und Meer baut er seine Ängste ab: »Ich möchte für immer hier wohnen, selbst wenn meine Beine nicht mehr mitmachen.«

Phare moderne ou tour enchantée ? Exercice avec des legos ou hommage totémique à la mystérieuse mer du Japon ?

Avec une vue imprenable sur le pont suspendu d'Akashi reliant la ville de Kobe à l'île d'Awaji, la maison 4 x 4 – ainsi appelée parce que cette tour comprend 4 niveaux faisant chacun 4 m² – est un chef-d'œuvre miniature. Tadao Ando l'a construite pour Yoshinari Nakata, architecte et promoteur. Ce dernier avait acheté 300 m² de terrain en bord de mer pour des raisons sentimentales : il était né sur l'île d'Awaji et y avait grandi. Le dernier étage fait saillie et est décalé d'un mètre par rapport aux autres étages afin de créer de l'espace pour un escalier. Au rez-de-chaussée, le hall d'entrée et la salle de bains, au premier étage, la chambre à coucher, au deuxième étage, le bureau ; et le salon et la cuisine au troisième étage. Pour Nakata, vivre dans cette tour a un effet anti-stress. Son angoisse diminue quand il perçoit les mouvements rythmiques du soleil et de la mer. « C'est ici que je veux vivre à tout jamais même si mes jambes me trahissent. »

※ **ABOVE** The living area and kitchen with a full plate glass wall afford stunning vistas of the Akashi bridge and the Inland Sea. **LEFT** Yoshinari Nakata in his living room. **FACING PAGE** The top storey of the 4 x 4 house juts out to sea. ※ **OBEN** Wohnzimmer und Küche bieten durch ein Fenster, das eine ganze Wand einnimmt, wunderbare Sicht auf die Akashi-Brücke und die Inland-See. **LINKS** Yoshinari Nakata in seinem Wohnzimmer. **RECHTE SEITE** Die oberste Etage des 4 x 4-Hauses ragt auf die Inland-See hinaus. ※ **CI-DESSUS** La paroi entièrement vitrée du salon et de la cuisine offre une vue imprenable sur le pont d'Akashi et la mer du Japon. **A GAUCHE** Yoshinari Nakata dans son salon. **PAGE DE DROITE** Le dernier étage de la Maison 4 x 4 s'élève au-dessus de la mer.

✳ **FACING PAGE** The bedroom closets are neatly fitted behind the futon. Ando designed the fittings and furniture. **ABOVE** The streamlined kitchen is of minimalist precision and detail. **FOLLOWING PAGES** A flat-screen television is the only artwork in the living room. ✳ **LINKE SEITE** Die Schlafzimmerschränke passen genau hinter den Futon. Ando entwarf die Einbauten und die Möbel. **OBEN** Die Kücheneinrichtung wurde auf ein Minimum reduziert, ohne auf das Wesentliche zu verzichten. **FOLGENDE DOPPELSEITE** Ein Flachbild-Fernseher ist das einzige Kunstwerk im Wohnzimmer. ✳ **PAGE DE GAUCHE** Les placards de la chambre à coucher sont parfaitement encastrés derrière le futon. Ando a dessiné les boiseries et le mobilier.. **CI-DESSUS** La cuisine épurée est d'une précision minimaliste. **DOUBLE PAGE SUIVANTE** un téléviseur à écran plat, seule concession à l'art, dans le salon.

BIBLIOGRAPHY

TIBET *
TRAVEL AND HOTEL GUIDES

FÖRST, HANS: Tibet Reiseführer – Land und Leute. Weishaupt.
  Gnas (Austria) 2002.

MAYHEW, BRADLEY: Tibet. Melbourne and London 2002.
  (*Lonely Planet*)

TIBET HANDBOOK. Bath. updated 2004. (*Footprint*)

TIBET * ILLUSTRATED BOOKS

BALDIZOINNE, TIZIANA AND GIANNI: Tibet: Journey to the
  Forbidden City (Photos and Text). Stewart, Tabori and Chang.
  New York 1996.

BEER, ROBERT: The Handbook of Tibetan Buddhist Symbols.
  Shambhala. Boston and London 2003.

CHAPMAN, WILLIAM: The Face of Tibet. Foreword by His Holiness
  the Dalai Lama. Georgia Press. Athens and London 2001.

DAVID-NOEL, ALEXANDRA: Mein Leben auf dem Dach der Welt.
  Droemer Knaur. München 2001.

DIE SYMBOLE DES TIBETISCHEN BUDDHISMUS.
  Diederichs. München 2003.

FISHER, ROBERT: Art of Tibet. Thames and Hudson. London 1997.

HUNTINGTON, JOHN AND BANGDAL, DINA: The Circle of Bliss:
  Buddhist Meditational Art. The Columbus Museum of Art. Columbus,
  Ohio 2004.

MATTHIEU, RICARD: Monk Dancers of Tibet.
  Shambhala. Boston and London 2003.

MCRAE: Shangrila – Die Suche nach dem letzten Paradies.
  Piper. München 2004.

PATTISON, ELLIOT: Der fremde Tibeter. Aufbau. Berlin 2003.

PEISSEL, MICHEL: Land ohne Horizonte. Malik. München 2004.

RHIE, MARILYN AND THURMAN, ROBERT: Wisdom and
  Compassion: The Sacred Art of Tibet. Harry Abrams. New York 1991.

SHASHIBALA: Buddhist Art: In Praise of the Divine.
  Roli and Janssen. New Delhi 2003.

TIBET * OTHER BOOKS

FRENCH, PATRICK: Tibet, Tibet: A Personal History of a Lost Land.
  HarperCollins. London 2003.

HARRER, HEINRICH: Sieben Jahre in Tibet. Ullstein. Berlin 1997.

HOPKIRK, PETER: Tresspassers On the Roof of the World:
  The Race for Lhasa. Oxford University Press. Oxford and London 2001.

LAMA, DALAI H.H. AND CUTLER, HOWARD: The Art of Happiness.
  Hodder and Stoughton. London 1999.
LAMA, DALAI H.H. AND VREELAND, NICHOLAS:
  An Open Heart: Practising Compassion in Everyday Life.
  Hodder and Stoughton. London 2001.
LAMA, DALAI H.H. AND HOPKINS, JEFFREY:
  Kalachakra Tantra: Rite of Initiation. Wisdom Publications. Boston 1999.

POMMARET, FRANÇOISE: Le Tibet. Une civilisation blessée.
  Gallimard. Paris 2002.

RAY, REGINALD: Indestructible Truth: The Living Spirituality of Tibetan
  Buddhism. Shambhala. Boston and London 2000.

THURMAN, ROBERT: Inner revolution. Life, Liberty and the Persuit of Real
  Happiness. Berkeley Pub. Group. New York 1999.
  Essential Tibetan Buddhism. Book Sales. New York 1997.
  Infinite Life. Seven Virtues of Living Well. Putnam P. G. New York 2004.

NEPAL *
TRAVEL AND HOTEL GUIDES

AUBERT, HANS-JOACHIM: Nepal.
  DuMont. Köln 2001. (*DuMont Reisebücher*)

KRACK, RAINER: Nepal. Bielefeld 2002. (*Reise Know-How Verlag*)

MAYHEW, BRADLEY ET AL: Nepal. Melbourne and London 2003.
  (*Lonely Planet*)

REED, DAVID Nepal. Berlin 2000. (*Stefan Loose Travel Handbücher*)

WIESMER: Nepal – Götter, Tempel und Paläste. DuMont. Köln 1997.

WOODHATCH: Nepal Handbook. Bath 1999. (*Footprint*)

NEPAL * ILLUSTRATED BOOKS

AMIN, MOHAMED (PHOTOS), WILLETS, DUNCAN AND TETLEY,
  BRIAN (TEXT): Journey through Nepal. Camerapix International.
  Nairobi, Kenya 1993.

GUNTON, DENNIS: Lands of the Himalayas. Timeless Books. New Delhi 1995.

LLOYD, IAN (PHOTOS); MOORE, WENDY (TEXT): Kathmandu: The Forbidden Valley. Time Books International. New Delhi 1990.

SJB RANA, PRABHAKAR ET AL (TEXT); PANJIAR, PRASHANT (PHOTOS): The Ranas of Nepal. Timeless Books. New Delhi 2003.

THROUGH NEPAL. Camerapix Publishers International. Nairobi, 1993.

NEPAL * OTHER BOOKS

HILLARY, SIR EDMUND: View From the Summit: Fiftieth Anniversary of the Conquest of Everest. Corgi Books. London 2000.

KRAKAUER, JON: Into thin Air. A personal Account of the Mount Everest Disaster. Villard. New York 1997.

SCOTT, DOUG: Himalayan Climber: A Lifetime's quest to the World's Greatest Ranges. Sierra Club Books. San Francisco 1992.

INDIA * TRAVEL AND HOTEL GUIDES

ABRAM, DAVID ET AL: Indien. Der Süden. Köln 2002. Indien. Der Nordwesten. Köln 2003. (*Sefan Loose Travel Handbücher*)

BRADNOCK: India Handbook. Bath 2004 (*Footprint*)
INDIEN. Baedeker Verlag. Ostfildern 2003. (*Baedeker Allianz Reiseführer*)

MICHELL, GEORGE: Southern India. W.W. Norton. New York 1997. (*Blue Guide*)

SAWDAY, ALASTAIR: Special places to stay-in India. Sawday. Bristol 2003.

SINGH, SARINA ET AL: India. Melbourne and London 2003. (*Lonely Planet*)

INDIA * ILLUSTRATED BOOKS

BHARADWAY, MONISHA: Inside India – quintessential Indian style. Roli Books. London 1998.

BOSE, BIRAJ ET AL: L'Inde. Editions de Lodi. Paris 2004.

IMBER, WALTER, BOESCH, HANS: Indien. Kümmerly & Frey. Bern 1992.

LESAGE, MARION ET AL: L'Inde à fleur d'âmes. Editions de la Martinière. Paris 2004.

MARTINELLI, ANTONIO (PHOTOS), MICHELL, GEORGE (TEXT): The Royal Palaces of India. Thames and Hudson. London 1997.

MICHAUD, SABRINA & ROLAND: Le voyage des Indes. Imprimerie nationale. Paris 2003.

NEUMANN-ADRIAN, EDDA & MICHAEL: Zeit für Indien – 30 Traumziele zum Wohlfühlen. Bucher. München 2002.

TASCHEN, ANGELIKA (EDITOR); VON SCHAEWEN, DEIDI; (PHOTOS) SETHI, SUNIL (TEXT): Indian Interiors. Taschen. Cologne 2000.

TASCHEN, ANGELIKA (EDITOR), REITER, CHRISTIANE (TEXT): The Hotel Book. Great Escapes Asia. Taschen. Cologne 2004.

WILSON, HENRY: India: Decoration Interiors Design. Conran Octopus. London 2001.

INDIA * OTHER BOOKS

ALTMANN, ANDREAS: Notbremse nicht zu früh ziehen! Mit dem Zug durch Indien. Rowohlt. Reinbek 2003.

COLLINS, LARRY; LAPIERRE, DOMINIQUE: Gandhi. Um Mitternacht die Freiheit. Bertelsmann. Gütersloh 1983

DALRYMPLE, WILLIAM: White Mughals. HarperCollins. London 2002.

FISHLOCK, TREVOR: Cobra Road: An Indian Journey. John Murray. London 1999.

FORSTER, E.M.: A Passage to India. Harvest Books. London 1984.

HESSE, HERMANN: Aus Indien. Suhrkamp. Frankfurt 1980. Siddharta. Suhrkamp. Frankfurt 1999.

IRVING, JOHN: Son of the Circus. Corgi Adult. Sidney 1995. Zirkuskind. Diogenes. Zürich 2000.

LAPIERRE, DOMINIQUE: Stadt der Freude. Bertelsmann. Gütersloh 1996.

NAIPAUL, V.S.: India. A wounded Civilization. Vintage Books. New York 2003.

ROY, ARUNDHATI: The God of Small Things. Penguin Books (India) 2002.

RUSHDIE, SALMAN: Midnight's Children. Granta. London 1990. Mitternachtskinder. Piper. München 1992.

SETH, VIKRAM: A suitable Boy. Perennial. New York 2003.

BIBLIOGRAPHY

SHASHI, THAROOR: Indien - Zwischen Mythos und Moderne. Insel. Frankfurt/M. 2000. From midnight to millenium. Arcade. New York.

TAGORE, RABINDRANAGH: My Reminiscences. Pan Macmillan. London 1991.

Sri Lanka * Travel and Hotel Guides

BRADNOCK, ROBERT: Sri Lanka Handbook. Bath 2001. (*Footprint*)

KRACK, RAINER: Sri Lanka. Bielefeld 2004. (*Reise Know-How*)

PLUNKETT, RICHARD AND ELLEMOR, BRIGITTE: Sri Lanka. Melbourne and London 2003. (*Lonely Planet*)

SRI LANKA 2004/2005. Berlin & München. (*Polyglott/ APA Guide*)

Sri Lanka * Illustrated Books

BECHERT AND GOMBRICH: The World of Buddism. Thames and Hudson. London 1991.

DIE WELT DES BUDDHISMUS. Orbis. München 2002.

GARRAULT, EDITH: Broder l'Asie. Hors Collection. Paris 2003.

ORTNER, JON; KORNFIELD, JACK (INTROD.): Buddha. Welcome Books. New York 2003.

ROBSON, DAVID: Geoffrey Bawa: The Complete Works. Thames and Hudson. London 2002.

Sri Lanka * Other Books

GUNESEKARA, ROMESH: Heaven's Edge. Bloomsbury. London 2002.

ONDAATJE, MICHAEL: Anil's Ghost. Vintage International. New York 2001.

Myanmar * Travel and Hotel Guides

BIRMA (MYANMAR). Singapore (GB) Berlin u. München (D) 2003/2004. (*Polyglott/ APA Guide*)

MARKAND, A.&M.; PETRICH, MARTIN H; KLINKMÜLLER, VOLKER: Myanmar. Berlin 2003. (*Stefan Loose Travel Handbücher*)

MARTIN, STEVEN: Myanmar (Burma). Melbourne and London 2002. (*Lonely Planet*)

Myanmar * Illustrated Books

DELL, ELIZABETH AND DUDLEY, SANDRA (EDITOR): Textiles from Burma. Philip Wilson Publishers. London 2003.

Myanmar * Other Books

GHOSH, AMITAV: The Glass Palace. HarperCollins. London 2001.

SUU KYI, AUNG SAN: Freedom from Fear and Other Writings.

Thailand * Travel and Hotel Guides

CUMMINGS, JOE ET AL: Thailand. Melbourne and London 2003. (*Lonely Planet*)

DORING, R., LOOSE, R.U.S., SPRAUL-DORING, U.: Thailand. Berlin 2003. (*Stefan Loose Travel Handbücher*)

DÜKER, J. (ED.): Südostasien – Thailand, Laos, Kambodscha, Vietnam. Berlin 2004. (*Stefan Loose Travel Handbücher*)

GRAY, PAUL: The Rough Guide to Thailand. London 2002. (*Rough Guides*)

THAILAND. Baedeker Verlag Ostfildern 2002. (*Baedeker Allianz Reiseführer*)

Thailand * Illustrated Books

CONVAY, SUSAN: Thai Textiles. Museum Press. London 2001.

DEVAHASTIN NA AYUDHYA, WONGVIPA AND MARSDEN, JANE

DOUGHTY (TEXT); TETTONI, LUCA INVERNIZZI (PHOTOS): Contemporary Thai. Periplus Editions. Hong Kong 2000.

WARREN, WILLIAM: Arts and Crafts of Thailand. Thames and Hudson. London 1994.

THAILAND * OTHER BOOKS

HAUSEMER, GEORGES: Der lächelnde Elefant in der Rushour.
Thailändische Szenerien. Picus. Wien 2002.

SMITH DOW, LESLIE: Anna Leonowens: A Life Beyond "the King and I".
Pottersfield. 1992.

WARREN, WILLIAM: Jim Thompson: The Unsolved Mystery.
Archipelago. Singapore 1998.

LAOS * TRAVEL AND HOTEL GUIDES

DUSIK, ROLAND: Laos-Kambodscha.
DuMont. Köln 2003. (*DuMont Richtig Reisen*)

ELIOT, BICKERSTETH, GILMORE: Laos Handbook.
Bath 2002. (*Footprint*)

PETRICH, MARTIN H.: Vietnam, Kambodscha und Laos. DuMont Köln
2004. (*DuMont Kunstreiseführer*)

LAOS *ILLUSTRATED BOOKS

BROCHEUX, PIERRE ; HEMERY, DANIEL : Indochine.
La Colonisation ambiguë, 1858–1954. Editions La Découverte. Paris 2004.

ENGELMANN, FRANCIS: Luang Prabang, Capitale de Légende.
ASA èditions. Paris 1997.

GITEAU, MADELEINE: Art et archéologie du Laos. Picard. Paris. 2001.

UNGER, ANN: Laos – Land zwischen gestern und morgen. Hirmer.
München 1995

LAOS * OTHER BOOKS

GOSLING, BETTY: Old Luang Prabang.
Oxford University Press. Kuala Lumpur 1996.

KOTTE, SIEBERT: Laos – Aufbruch am Mekong.
Horlemann. Bad Honnef 2002.

STUART-FOX, MARTIN: The Lao Kingdom of Lan Xang: Rise and Decline.
White Lotus. Bangkok 1998.

CAMBODIA * TRAVEL AND HOTEL GUIDES

RAY, NICK: Cambodia. Melbourne and London 2002.
(*Lonely Planet*)

CAMBODIA * ILLUSTRATED BOOKS

COE, MICHAEL: Angkor and the Khmer Civilization.
Thames & Hudson. London 2003.

ORTNER, JON (PHOTOS); MABBETT, IAN ET AL (TEXT):
Angkor, Celestial Temples of the Khmer Empire. Abbeville Press.
New York and London 2002.

RIBOUD, MARC (PHOTOS), LACOUTURE, JEAN ET AL (TEXT):
Angkor: The Serenity of Buddhism. Thames and Hudson. London 1993.

CAMBODIA * OTHER BOOKS

BECKER, ELIZABETH: When the War was Over. Public Affairs. Perseus
Books Group. New York 1998.

LEWIS, NORMAN: A Dragon apparent. Eland. London 2003.

LOUNG, UNG: First They Killed My Father: A Daughter of Cambodia
Remembers. HarperCollins. New York 2000.

SINGAPORE * TRAVEL AND HOTEL GUIDES

LOOSE, R. & .S.: Malaysia, Burnei, Singapur. Berlin 2004.
(*Stefan Loose Travel Handbücher*)

PETERS, ED AND CHAN, JOHN: Insight Guide Asia's Best Hotels
and Resorts. Singapore 2003. (*Apa Guide*)

RICHMOND, SIMON: Malaysia, Singapore and Brunei.
Melbourne and London 2004. (*Lonely Planet*)

SINGAPORE * ILLUSTRATED BOOKS

POWELL, ROBERT (TEXT); BINGHAM-HALL, PATRICK (PHOTOS):
Singapore Architecture: A Short History. Periplus. Hong Kong 2004.

BiBLiOGRApHY

Singapore * Other Books

BARLEY, NIGEL: Der Löwe von Singapore. Klett, London 1996.

MORLEY, JOHN DAVID: Nach dem Monsun.
Eine Kindheit in den britischen Kolonien. Malik. München 2001.

Malaysia * Travel and Hotel Guides

RICHMOND, SIMON: Malaysia, Singapore and Brunei.
Melbourne and London 2004. (*Lonely Planet*)

Malaysia * Illustrated Books

BEAL, GILLIAN (TEXT); TERMANSEN, JACOB; MOLBECH,
PIA MARIE (PHOTOS): Tropical Style. Periplus. Hong Kong 2003.

Malaysia * Other Books

BURGESS, ANTHONY: The Malayian Trilogy. Vintage Classics.
London 2000.

RASLAN, KARIM: Journeys Through Southeast Asia.
Times Books International. Singapore and Kuala Lumpur 2002.

Indonesia * Travel and Hotel Guides

DALY, KATE: Bali. Melbourne and London 2003. (*Lonely Planet Publications*)

ELIOT, JISHUA: Indonesia Handbook. Bath 2002. (*Footprint*)

LOOSE, R & S: Indonesien. Berlin 2002. (*Stefan Loose Travel Handbücher*)

SEKI, AKIHIKO: Bali Resort and Spa (Asia Shifuku no Resort).
Tokimeki Publishing. Japan 2003.

TURNER, PETER: Java. Melbourne and London 1999. (*Lonely Planet*)

WITTON, PATRICK ET AL: Indonesia.
Melbourne and London 2003. (*Lonely Planet*)

Indonesia * Illustrated Books

BEAL, GILLIAN (TEXT); TERMANSEN, JACOB (PHOTOS):
Island Style. Periplus Editions. Hong Kong 2002.

DAVISON, JULIAN (TEXT); TETTONI, LUCA INVERNIZZI
(PHOTOS): Introduction to Balinese Architecture. Periplus Editions.
Hong Kong 2003.

GINANNESCHI, ISABELLA (PHOTOS); WIJAYA MADE (TEXT):
At Home in Bali. Abbeville Press. New York 2000.

HELMI, RIO (PHOTOS); WALKER, BARBARA (TEXT):
Bali Style: Vendome. New York 2000.

TEGGIA GABRIELLA; HANUSZ MARK: Indonesia.
A cup of Java (Losari Coffee Plantation). Equinox. London 2003.

Indonesia * Other Books

CONRAD, JOSEPH: Lord Jim. Penguin. London 1989.
Lord Jim. Piper. München 1989.

MULTATULI: Max Havelaar or The Coffee Auctions of the Dutch Trading
Company. Penguin. London 1991.
Max Havelaar oder Die Kaffeeversteigerung der Niederländischen
Handelsgesellschaft. Ullstein. Berlin 1997.

NOOTEBOOM, CEES: Im Frühling der Tau. Suhrkamp. Frankfurt 1997.
Du printemps, la rosée. (Voyages en Extrême-Orient).
Actes Sud. Arles 1999.

ROWTHORN, CHRIS ET AL: South-east Asia on a Shoestring.
Melbourne and London 2001. (*Lonely Planet*)

TOER, PRAMOEDYA ANANTA: Child of All Nations.
Penguin. London 1996.
Kind aller Völker. Unionsverlag. München 1994.

TOURNIER, MICHEL: Vendredi ou les limbes du Pacifique.
Edition Flammarion. Paris 1995.
Vendredi ou la vie sauvage. Edition Gallimard. Paris 1987.

VICKERS, ADRIAN: Bali: A Paradise Created.
Tuttle. Boston 1996.
Ein Paradies wird erfunden. Geschichte einer kulturellen Begegnung.
Reise Know How. Bielefeld 1996.

Philippines * Travel and Hotel Guides

DUSIK, ROLAND: Philippinen. DuMont. Köln 1997.
(*DuMont Richtig Reisen*)

KERR, RUSS ET AL: Philippines. Melbourne and London 2000.
(*Lonely Planet*)

SCHAEFER, ALBRECHT: Philippinen. Edition Erde Temmen. Bremen 1995.

PHILIPPINES * ILLUSTRATED BOOKS

REYES, ELIZABETH (TEXT), ONG, CHESTER (PHOTOS):
Tropical Interiors: Contemporary Dream Houses in the Philippines.
Periplus. Hong Kong 2000.

PHILIPPINES * OTHER BOOKS

GARLAND, ALEX: The Tesseract. Penguin. London 1999.
Manila. Goldmann. München 2001.

Vietnam * TRAVEL AND HOTEL GUIDES

MASON, FLORENCE: Hanoi. Melbourne and London. 1999. (*Lonely Planet*)
Vietnam. Melbourne and London 2003. (*Lonely Planet*)
Vietnam. Travel Handbuch. Köln 2001. (*Stefan Loose Travel Handbücher*)

SHIOZAWA, SHIN: Vietnam - 32 Hip Hotels and 13 Travel Points.
Tokyo 2002. (*Up Front Books*)

VIETNAM. Singapore (GB) 2000, Berlin u. München (D) 2000.
(*Polyglott/ APA Guide*)

Vietnam * ILLUSTRATED BOOKS

FITZGERALD, FRANCES (TEXT), CROSS, MARY (PHOTOS):
Vietnam: Spirits of the Earth. Bulfinch Press. USA 2001.

QUAN, NGUYEN ET ALT.: Vietnam.
Portraits and Landscapes. Stemmle. Zürich 2002.

Vietnam * OTHER BOOKS

CHONG, DENISE: The Girl in the Picture: The Story of Kim Phuc.
Penguin. London 2001.
Das Mädchen hinter dem Foto. Lübbe. Bergisch-Gladbach 2003.
La fille de la photo. Gallimard. Paris 2000.

DUONG, THU HUONG: Paradise of the Blind. HarperCollins.
New York 1993.

ELLIOTT, DUONG VAN MAI:
The Sacred Willow: Four Generations in the Life of a Vietnamese Family.
Oxford University Press. New York and Oxford 1999.

KARNOW, STANLEY: Vietnam: A History.
Penguin. New York 1983.

KOTTE, HEINZ; SIEBERT, RÜDIGER: Vietnam – die neue Zeit auf 100
Uhren. Lamm. Göttingen 2001.

LAMB, DAVID: Vietnam, Now: A Reporter Returns.
PublicAffairs. New York 2002.

THICH NHAT HANH: Der Mondbambus. Droemer Knaur. München 2002.

HONG KONG * TRAVEL AND HOTEL GUIDES

LIPS, WERNER: Hongkong, Macau, Kanton.
Bielefeld 2002. (*Reise-Know-How*)

WITTON, PATRICK: Hong Kong Condensed.
Melbourne and London 2003. (*Lonely Planet*)

HONG KONG * ILLUSTRATED BOOKS

BENGE, SOPHIE (TEXT); VON DER SCHULENBERG,
FRITZ (PHOTOS): Private Hong Kong: Where East Meets West.
Abbeville Press. New York and London 1997.

HONG KONG * OTHER BOOKS

HANIG, FLORIAN: Der Buddha in der 42. Etage, Asiatische Metropolen.
Picus. Wien 2001.

NEBENZAL, HAROLD: Hafen der Düfte oder
Die letzten Tage von Hongkong. Heyne. München 2001.

OKAKURA, KAKUZO: Das Buch vom Tee. Insel. Frankfurt/M. 2002.

CHINA * TRAVEL AND HOTEL GUIDES

CHEN, HANNE: Kulturschock China.
Bielefeld 2004. (*Reise-Know-How*)

GUIDE BLEU: Chine, de Pékin à Hong Kong.
Hachette Tourisme. Paris 2003. (*Guides Bleus*)

HARPER, DAMIAN: China.
Melbourne and London 2002. (*Lonely Planet*)

LEFFMANN, DAVID ET AL: China. Der Osten. Berlin 2003.
(*Stefan Loose Travel Handbücher*)

MAYHEW, BRADLEY: Shanghai.
Melbourne and London 2004. (*Lonely Planet*)

MILLER, KORINNA: Best of Beijing.
Melbourne and London 2004. (*Lonely Planet*)

BiBLiOgraphy

China * ILLUStrated BOOKS

CHAN TAT CHUEN, WILLIAM: A la table de l'empereur de Chine. Editions Philippe Picquier. Arles 2002.

LEECE, SHARON (TEXT); ONG, CHESTER (PHOTOS): China Modern. Periplus Editions. Hong Kong 2003.

MIN, ANCHEE ET AL: Chinese Propaganda Posters: From the Collection of Michael Wolf. Taschen. Cologne 2003.

China * Other BOOKS

CHANG, JUNG: Wild Swans: Three Daughters of China. Flamingo. London 1993. Wilde Schwäne. Droemer Knaur. München 2003.

CHAN TAT CHUEN, WILLIAM : Fêtes et banquets en Chine. Editions Philippe Picquier. Arles 1992.

DAN, SHI: Mémoires d'un eunuque dans la cité interdite. Editions Philippe Picquier. Arles 1999.

GERNET, JACQUES: Die chinesische Welt. Suhrkamp. Frankfurt 1988.

HA, JIN: Waiting. Vintage. Anchor Books Doubleday. New York 2002.

HUI, WEI: Shanghai Baby. Ullstein. München 2004.

JAVARY, CYRILLE: Dans la cité pourpre interdite. Editions Philippe Picquier. Arles 2001.

JIN, YI: Mémoires d'une dame de cour dans la cité interdite. Editions Philippe Picquier. Arles 1998.

LI, ZHISUI: The Private Life of Chairman Mao: The Memoirs of Mao's Personal Physician. Random House. New York 1996.

MAASS, HARALD, WEI, LI: Kinder des Himmlischen Friedens. Frederking & Thaler München 2002.

NAMU: Leaving Mother Lake. Abacus. London 2003. Das Land der Töchter. Ullstein 2003.

PIMPANEAU, JACQUES: Lettre à une jeune fille qui voudrait partir en Chine. Editions Philippe Picquier. Arles 2001.

POLO, MARCO: Die Wunder der Welt. Insel. Frankfurt 2004.

SALISBURY, HARRISON: The New Emperors: Mao and Deng. HarperCollins. London 1993.

SEAGRAVE, STERLING: Dragon Lady: The Life and Legend of the Last Empress of China. Alfred A. Knopf. New York 1992.

SETH, VIKRAM: From Heaven Lake: Travels in Sinkiang and Tibet. Chatto and Windus. London 1983.

SPENCER, JONATHAN: The search for modern China. Norton. NY 1990. Chinas Weg in die Moderne. Nauser. München 1995.

STRITTMATTER, KAI: Vorwärts, Genossen! Chinesische Sternenfischer. Picus Verlag Wien 2003.

WENFU, LU: Der Gourmet. Diogenes. Zürich 2001. Vie et passion d'un gastronome chinois. Editions Philippe Picquier. Arles 1988.

Japan * Travel and Hotel Guides

ASHBURNE, JOHN: Tokyo Condensed. Melbourne and London 2002. (Lonely Planet)

CHIKYU NO ARUKIKATA (EDITITING TEAM): Penang, Lankaui, Tioman, Pankor – Chikyu No Arukikata Resort. Diamond Big Sha. Tokyo 2003.

EYEWITNESS DK: Japan. DK. London 2002.

JAPAN. Singapore (GB) 2003, Berlin u. München (D) 2003. (Polyglott/ APA Guide)

MIYOSHI, KAZUYOSHI: Okinawa – Nirai Kanai Kami no Sumu Rakuen. Shogakukan Tokyo 2002. Japanese Paradise (Wa no Rakuen – Nippon no Yado). Shogakukan. Tokyo 1999.

ROWTHORN, CHRIS: Japan. Melbourne and London 2003. (Lonely Planet)

VIS À VIS: Japan. DK. München 2003.

Japan * ILLUStrated BOOKS

ANDO, TADAO AND DAL CO, FRANCESCO: The Complete Works. Phaidon Press. London 1995.

BASSET, ALAIN: Japon. Les délices de l'extrême. Renaissance du Livre. Tournai 2004.

BOUTONNAT, LOUISE ET KUSHIZAKI, HARUMI: La voie de l'encens. Editions Philippe Picquier. Arles 2000.

DURSTON, DIANA (TEXT), FUJII, LUCY BIRMIGHAM: The Living Traditions of Old Kyoto. Kodansha International. Tokyo and New York 1994.

FREEMAN, MICHAEL (PHOTOS); RICO NOSE, MICHIKO (TEXT):
Japan Modern: New Ideas for Contemporary Living.
Periplus Editions. Hong Kong 2000.

KEANE, OHASHI: L'Art du jardin au Japon.
Editions Philippe Picquier. Arles 1999.

MURATA, NOBORU (PHOTOS); BLACK, ALEXANDRA (TEXT):
The Japanese House. Tuttle Publishing. Boston and Tokyo 2000.

MURAMATSU; TOMOMI: Tawaraya, une auberge traditionnelle aules
traditionsvivantes du Japon. Editions Philippe Picquier. Arles 2002.

NITSCHKE, GUNTER: Japanese Gardens. Taschen. Cologne 2003.

Japan * Other Books

ABE, KOBO: The Woman in the Dunes. Vintage. New York 1991.
Die Frau in den Dünen. DTV. München 1992.
La femme des sables. Stock. 2002.

BRAZELL, KAREN (ED. & TRANSL.): Confessions of Lady Nijo.
Stanford University Press. 1982.

CLAVELL, JAMES: Shogun. Blanvelet. Berlin 2002.
Gai-Jin. Blanvelet. Berlin 2003
COBB, DAVID (EDITOR): Haiku. The British Museum Press. London 2002.

GOLDEN, ARTHUR: Memoirs of a Geisha.
Random House. New York 1998.
Die Geisha. Goldmann. München 2004.
Geisha. J.–C. Lattès. Paris 1999.

IWASAKI, MINEKO: Die wahre Gechichte der Geisha.
Heyne. München 2003.

KAWABATA, YASUNARI: The Dancing Girl of Izu.
Counterpoint Press. USA 2002.
Die Tänzerin von Izu. Hanser. München 1968.
La Danseuse d'Izu. Albin Michel. Paris 1973.

KERR, ALEX: Lost Japan. Lonely Planet. Melbourne and London 1996.
Dogs and Demons: Tales from the Dark Side of Japan. New York 2001.

MISHIMA, YUKIO: Forbidden Colours. Secker and Warburg. London 1968.
Schnee im Frühling. Hanser. Hamburg 1985.

MORLEY, JOHN DAVID: Grammatik des Lächelns. Piper. München 2003.

MURAKAMI, HARUKI: South of the Border, West of the Sun.
Vintage. New York 2003.
Naokos Lächeln. Goldmann. München 2003.
Au sud de la frontière, à l'ouest du soleil. Belfond. Paris 2002.

MURASAKI, SHIKIBU: Die Geschichte vom Prinzen Genji.
Insel. Frankfurt/M. 1995.

OE, KENZABURO: A Personal Matter. Grove Press. New York 1988.
Eine persönliche Erfahrung. Suhrkamp. Frankfurt/M. 2000.
Une affaire personelle. Stock. Paris 2000.

RICHIE, DONALD: The Inland Sea.
Stone Bridge Press. Berkeley, California 2002.

SMITH, PATRICK: Japan: A Reinterpretation.
Pantheon. New York 1997.

TSUNOI, NAOKO ET AL: 100 regards inédits sur le Japon et 1000 bonnes
adresses japonaises en France. Jipango. Paris 2004.

Books on Feng Shui

FRÖHLING, THOMAS; MARTIN, KATRIN: Wohnen mit Feng Shui.
Bassermann. München 2004.

LAMBERT, MARY; SKINNER, STEPHEN: Feng Shui.
Orbis. München 2002.

MAININI, SIMONA F.: Feng Shui for Architecture.
Xlibris Corporation. Philadelphia 2004.

O'BRIEN, SOPHIE: Feng Shui in the Home: Creating Harmony.
Periplus Editions. Hong Kong 2002.

SATOR, GÜNTHER: Feng Shui, Leben und Wohnen in Harmonie.
Gräfe & Unzer. München 2004.

SKINNER, STEPHEN: Flying Star Feng Shui.
Tuttle. Boston and Rutland, Vermont 2003.

STASNEY, SHARON: Feng Shui Living. Chapelle. USA 2003.

TOO, LILLIAN: Easy-to-Use Feng Shui. Collins and Brown. London 1999.
Die Grundlagen des Feng Shui. Droemer Knaur. München 2000.

WONG, EVA: A Master Course in Feng-Shui. Shambhala. Boston 2001.

ADDRESSES

MONASTERIES
INDIA

PEMAYANGTSE MONASTERY
West Sikkim
Two hour bus ride from Gangtok.
For more information contact:
Muyal Liang Trust
53 Blenheim Crescent
London W11 2EG
United Kingdom
tel: + 44 (207) 229 4774

PADMANABHAPURAM PALACE
Nagercoil
Tamil Nadu
Open from 9 am to 4.30 pm from
Tuesday to Saturday

RUMTEK MONASTERY
Gangtok
Sikkim
www.rumtek.org
Open from 8 am to 5 pm daily in summer
and from 10 am to 5 pm in winter.

CAMBODIA

WAT DAMNAK
The Center of Khmer Studies
Siem Reap
PO Box 9380
tel. + 855 (063) 96 4385
email: center@khmerstudies.org
www.khmerstudies.org

HOTELS
INDIA

SHIV NIWAS PALACE (Vol. I, page 114)
The City Palace
Udaipur 313001
Rajasthan, India
tel: +91 (294) 2 5280 1619
fax: +91 (294) 252 8006
email: crs@udaipur.hrhindia.com
www.hrhindia.com

THE MALABAR HOUSE (Vol. I, page 134)
1/268 and 1/269 Parade Road
Fort Cochin 682 001
Kerala, India
tel: +91 (484) 21 6666

fax: +91 (484) 21 7777
email: info@malabarhouse.com
www.malabarhouse.com

SRI LANKA

APA VILLA (Vol. I, page 140)
78th Mile Post
Matara Road
Thalpe
Galle, Sri Lanka
tel./fax: +94 (91) 228 3320
tel: +94 (91) 228 2372

ILLUKETIA (Vol. I, page 146)
Illuketia
Elluketiya Watta
Wanchawala
Galle, Sri Lanka
tel: +94 (91) 438 1411
Contact for both properties:
Nikki Harrison: tel/fax: +94 (91) 228 3320
mobile: +94 7 7731 7299
Hans Höfer: hoefer@pacific.net.sg
email: villa-srilanka@sltnet.lk, harrison@sri.lanka.net
www.villa-srilanka.com

MYANMAR

BAGAN HOTEL (Vol. I, page 172)
Bagan
Old Bagan, Myanmar
tel: +95 (2) 6 7145
fax: +95 (2) 6 7311
e-mail: olbagho@bagan.net.mm
www.myanmars.net/baganhotel

INLE PRINCESS RESORT (Vol. I, page 192)
Sales and Reservations Office
21-22 Bahosi Complex, Suite B-3
Bogyoke Aung San Street
Lanmadaw Township
Yangon, Myanmar
tel. +95 (1) 21 1226
fax. +95 (1) 21 0972
email: princess@yangon.net.mm
www.inleprincessresort.com

THAILAND

SWAIRIANG GUESTHOUSE (Vol. I, page 232)
308 Chiangmai-Lamphun Road
Sarapee Chiangmai 50140
tel: +66 (53) 32 2061
fax: +66 (53) 32 2062

email: info@swairiang.com
www.swairing.com

GOLDEN NAGA BARGE (Vol. I, page 238)
J.M. Beurdeley
30 Ramkamheng Soi 24
Bangkok 10240
tel/fax: + 66 (2) 718 5521
email: jmbeurdeley@yahoo.com

THE MAHA BHETRA (Vol. I, page 262)
Frederic Varnier
Amanpuri Hotel
116/1 Srisconthorn Road
A.Thalang, Phuket
tel: +66 (76) 32 4333
fax: +66 (76) 27 0400
email: amanpuri@amanresorts.com

LAOS

BOUTIQUE HOTEL LES 3 NAGAS
(Vol. I, page 284)
Ban Vat Nong
P.O. Box 722
Luang Prabang
Lao P.D.R.
tel: +856 (71) 25 3888
fax: +856 (71) 25 3999
email: info@3nagas.com
www.3nagas.com

CAMBODIA

AMANSARA (Vol. I, page 356)
Road to Angkor
Siem Reap
Kingdom of Cambodia
tel. +855 (63) 76 0333
fax. +855 (63) 76 0335
email: amansara@amanresorts.com
tel. +855 (65) 6887 3337
fax. +855 (65) 6887 3338
email: reservations@amanresorts.com
www.amanresorts.com

SINGAPORE

THE CHINA CLUB SINGAPORE
(Vol. I, page 364)
China Club Investment Pte Ltd
168 Robinson Road
52/F Capital Tower
Singapore 068912
tel: +65 6820 2388

fax: +65 6820 2788
email: reservation@chinaclub.com.sg
www.chinaclub.com.sg

Malaysia

BLUE MANSION (Vol. I, page 412)
Cheong Fatt Tze Mansion
14 Leith Street, Georgetown
Penang 10200, Malaysia
tel. +60 (4) 262 5289, 262 0006
email: cftm@tm.net.my
www.cheongfatttzemansion.com

Indonesia

AMANJIWO (Vol. II, page 8)
Borobudur
Java, Indonesia
tel. +62 (293) 78 8333
fax. +62 (293) 78 8355
email: reservations@amanresorts.com
www.amanresorts.com

LOSARI COFFEE PLANTATION (Vol. II, page 30)
Desa Losari – Grabag
P.O. Box 108, Magelang 56100
Central Java, Indonesia
tel. +62 (298) 59 6333
fax. +62 (298) 59 2696
info@losaricoffeeplantation.com
www.losaricoffeeplantation.com

BEGAWAN GIRI ESTATE (Vol. II, page 44)
P.O. Box 54
Ubud 80571
Bali, Indonesia
tel. +62 (361) 97 8888
fax. +62 (361) 97 8889
email: reservations@begawan.com
www.begawan.com

LINDA GARLAND ESTATE (Vol. II, page 54)
Banjar Nyuh Kuning, Desa Mas
PO Box 196
Ubud 80571
Gianyar, Bali
tel: +62 (361) 97 4028
fax: +62 (361) 97 4029
email: info@lindagarland.com
www.lindagarland.com

ANNEKE'S GUESTHOUSE (Vol. II, page 120)
Anneke van Waesberghe

P.O. Box 21P
Ubud
Gianyar 80571
Bali, Indonesia
tel: +62 (361) 97 6631
fax: +62 (361) 97 6630
email: esp2000@indo.net.id
www.espritenomade.com

TAMAN BEBEK VILLAS (Vol. II, page 134)
Sayan, Ubud 80571
Bali, Indonesia
Owner: Made Wijaya
Manager: Leo Eka Wijaya
tel: +62 (361) 97 5385
fax: +62 (361) 97 6532
email: tbvbali@indo.net.id
info@tamanbebek.com
www.tamanbebek.com

TAMAN SELINI HOTEL (Vol. II, page 142)
Beach Bungalows
Desa Pemuteran, Gerogkak
Singaraja
Bali, Indonesia
Owner: Ediana Vourloumis
Manager: Sari Harahap
(mobile: + 62 813 3878 3434)
tel: +62 (362) 9 4746
fax: +62 (362) 9 3449
email: selini_bali@nagura.net
selinibalipmt@yahoo.com

BALI TROPICAL VILLAS
Anita Lococo
Villa Rentals and Property Specialists
Jl. Raya Seminyak 56
Seminyak, Bali, Indonesia
tel/fax: +62 (361)73 2083
mobile: +62 81 2380 0858
email: anita@bali-tropical-villas.com
www.bali-tropical-villas.com

Hong Kong

THE CHINA CLUB HONG KONG
(Vol. II, page 230)
Clarence Chan
Club Manager
13/F The Old Bank of China Building
Bank Street
Central Hong Kong
tel: +85 (2) 2840 0233 and 2521 8888
fax: +85 (2) 2522 8011
email: tccgm01@netvigator.com

China

THE BAMBOO HOUSE (Vol. II, page 242)
& THE FURNITURE HOUSE (Vol. II, page 250)
SOHO China Ltd.
SOHO New Town, Tower B, 18/F
88 Jianquo Road, Chaoyang District
Beijing 100022, People's Republic of China
tel: +86 (10) 6567 3333 ext. 326
fax: +86 (10) 6667 1064
email: wangchunlei@sohochina.com
www.sohochina.com

RED CAPITAL RESIDENCE (Vol. II, page 284)
No. 67 Dongsi Batiao,
Dongcheng District,
Beijing 100007, People's Republic of China
tel: +86 (10) 6402 7150 and 8403 5308
email: info@redcapitalclub.com.cn
www.redcapitalclub.com.cn

THE CHINA CLUB BEIJING (Vol. II, page 294)
No. 51 Xi Rong Xian Lane
Xi Dan Beijing 100031
People's Republic of China
tel: +86 (10) 6605 8435
fax: +86 (10) 6603 9594
email: tccbmem@public.bta.net.cn

GRAND HYATT SHANGHAI (Vol. II, page 310)
Jin Mao Tower
88 Century Boulevard Pudong
Shanghai 2001121
People's Republic of China
tel: +86 (21) 5049 1234
fax: +86 (21) 5049 1111
email: info@hyattshanghai.com
www.shanghai.grand.hyatt.com

FUCHUN RESORT (Vol. II, page 322)
Fuyang Section
Hangfu Yanjiang Road
Hangzhou
Zhejiang 311401
People's Republic of China
tel: +86 (571) 6346 1111
fax: +86 (571) 6346 1222
email: fuchunresort@lcpc.biz

Addresses

Japan

CHIIORI (Vol. II, page 342)
(We are not officially a hotel. But people can
stay if they contact us in advance.)
Tsurui 209
Higashi-Iya Yamason
Miyoshi-gun
Tokushima-ken
JAPAN 770 0206
tel: +81 (883) 88 5290
fax: + 81 (883) 88 5290
www.chiiori.org

ARCHITECTS THAILAND

Chulathat Kitibutr
Chiangmai Architects Collaborative
50 Rajadumnern Road
Chiangmai 50200/Thailand
tel: +66 (53) 21 2113
fax: +66 (53) 21 0549
email: Chulathat@yahoo.com

Singapore

Mok Wei Wei
W Architects Pte Ltd
179 River Valley Road, #05-06
Singapore 179033
tel: +65 6333 9913
fax : +65 6733 3366
email: office@w-architects.com.sg

Chan Soo Khian
SCDA ARCHITECTS Pte. Ltd.
No. 10 Teck Lim Road
Singapore 088386
tel: +65 6324 5458
fax: +65 6324 5450
email: scda@starhub.net.sg
www.scdaarchitects.com

Cheong Yew Kuan
AREA
45 Cantonment Road
Singapore 089748
tel: +65 735 5995
fax: +65 738 8295
email: area@indo.net.id

Indonesia

Jaya P. Ibrahim
Jaya & Associates
Jalan Erlangga V/18
Kebayoran Baru
Jakarta 12110/Indonesia
tel: +62 (21) 7279 2107
fax: + 62 (21) 7279 4084
email: jayaibrahim@jaya-associates.com

Philippines

Eduardo G. Calma
Lor Calma Design, Inc.
G/F State Condo
186 Salcedo Street
Legaspi Village
Makati City, Philippines 1229
tel: +63 (2) 816 7927
fax: +63 (2) 817 1998
email: lvlparch@info.com.ph

Ramon Antonio
Unit 1203, 139 Corporate Center
139 Valero Street, Salcedo Village
Makati City, Philippines 1227
tel: + 63 (2) 813 7330
fax + 63 (2) 813 7331
email: rrantonio@axti.com
pradci@pacific.net.ph

Budji C. Layug
Budji Layug Design Architects
235 Nicanor Garcia Avenue
Bel-Air II, Makati City, Philippines
tel: + 63 (2) 896 6358, 896 6395
fax: + 63 (2) 896 8348
email: budji@mozcom.com

Japan

Kengo Kuma
Kengo Kuma & Associates
2-24-8 Minamiaoyama Minatoku
Tokyo 107-0062
tel: + 81 (3) 5754 3222
fax: + 81 (3) 5754 3223
email: lemm@vc.kcom.ne.jp
tel: + 81 (3) 3401 7721
fax: + 81 (3) 3401 7778
email: kuma@ba2.so-net.ne.jp
www.02.so-net.ne.jp

Shigeru Ban Architects
5-2-4 Matsubara, Setagaya-ku
Tokyo 156-0043, Japan
tel: +81 (3) 3324 6760
fax: +81 (3) 3324 6789
email: SAB@tokyo.email.ne.jp
www.dnp.co.jp/millennium/SB/VAN.html

Tadao Ando
Tadao Ando Architect & Associates
5-23 Toyosaki 2-Chome
Kita-Ku
Osaka 531-0072, Japan
tel: +81 (6) 6375 1148
email: taaa@mx6.nisiq.net

Eizo Shiina Architect and Associates
4-6-17 Seijo Setagayaku
Tokyo 157-0066, Japan
tel: +81 (3) 3482 8333
fax: +81 (3) 3482 7333
email: eizo@e-shiina.com
www.e-shiina.com

Yoshifumi Nakamura
3-45-4-3F
Okusawa
Setagayaku,
Tokyo 158-0083, Japan
tel: + 81 (3) 5754 3222
fax: + 81 (3) 5754 3223
email: lemm@vc.kcom.ne.jp

FOR FURTHER INTERESTS IN ASIA

zapaimages / Livio Gerber
Beethovenstrasse 47
CH-8002 Zurich
tel: +41 (1) 201 0834
fax: +41 (1) 201 0835
email: livio.gerber@zapaimages.com
www.zapaimages.com

Travel Book Shop
Gisela Treichler
Rindermarkt 20
CH-8001 Zurich
tel: +41 (1) 252 3883
fax: +41 (1) 252 3832
email: info@travelbookshop.ch
www.travelbookshop.com

ACKNOWLEDGEMENTS

Reto Guntli

The photographer would like to thank everyone who invited him to his temple, monastery, hotel, guest house or private home featured. For their kind contributions during the realization of "Inside Asia", special thanks to: Katherine G. de Guzman, for opening many doors in Singapore and the Philippines; Anita Lococo, "Bali-Tropical-Villas", Bali, for showing me Indonesian homes and resorts; Marisa Viravaidya, Bangkok, for her help in Thailand; Livio Gerber, Zapaimages Zurich, for his co-ordinations back home; Agi Simões, Zurich, for his photo assistance on many trips to Asia; Monica Sue Hoffman and Livio Gerber for being crucial in my lifesaving mission from India to Zurich.

In Nepal thanks to:
Dubby Bhagat, Gautam S.J.B. Rana

In India thanks to:
Ramji and Benu Bharany, Vikram Goel, Philip Mathew, Amit and Diya Mathew, Dalip and Nandini Mehta, Rajiv Mehrotra, A.G.K. Menon, Oliver and Kitten Musker, Ratish Nanda, Dr. Rajaram Panda, Prem and Cristina Patnaik, Vivek Sahni, Ramesh Sharma, Nina Singh, Pincha Singh, Kunjo Tashi, Lea Terhune, Ramesh Tharakan.

In Sri Lanka thanks to:
C. Anjalendran, Hiran Cooray, Ambassador Gopal Gandhi, Mrs Tara Gandhi, Nikki Harrison.

In Myanmar thanks to:
Sally Baughen, Rahul Kulshreshta, Zaw Min Yu, U Ohn Maung, Ko Kyaw Zay Ya.

In Thailand thanks to:
Tanu Malakul Na Ayudhaya, Sri, Rai and Nicklas von Bueren, Susie Hansirisawasdi, Phairoj Kosumkachonki-at, Cristina Funes-Noppen, Amaradist Smuthkochorn.

In Laos thanks to:
Francis Engelmann, Pascal Trahan.

In Cambodia thanks to:
Toby Anderson, Pierre Carron, Olivier Piot.

In Singapore thanks to:
Pacita Abad, Rita Iskander de Braux, Jack Garitty, Ila Ghose, Bridget Goh, Katherine G. de Guzman, Renato T. de Guzman, Nicholas Lee, Margaret Lum, Anjali Puri Rizvi and Rafat Rizvi, Prema Vishwanathan.

In Malaysia thanks to:
Edric Ong, Karim Raslan, Valentine Willie.

In Indonesia thanks to:
Carmanita, Isabella Ginanneschi, Daniela Gazzini, Joost van Grieken, Michelle Han, Jaya Ibrahim, Kamal Kaul, Asmeen Khan, Cheong Yew Kuan, Ambassador Edward Lee and Mrs. Sonia Lee, Ratina Moegiono, Pincky and Teguh Osternik, Tengku Ariatna H. Pongai and Benjamin A. Pongai, Arinto Prakoso, Setyanto P. Santosa, Ambassador Shyam Saran and Mrs. Anita Saran, John Saunders, Amar Sinha, Hudy M. Suharnoko, Tjetjep Suparman, Arun and Nina Taneja, Soma Temple, Anneke van Waesberghe, Christine Walker, Alec Wong, Adrian Zecha, Daphne Zepos.

In the Philippines thanks to:
Ramon Antonio, Bonjin Bolinao, Eduardo Calma, Budji Layug, George T. Goduco, Leandro Y. Locsin, Yolanda Perez Johnson and Patrick Johnson, Raul T. Manzano, Antonio Carlos Rodriguez Mendoza, Cora Relova and Ricky Toledo, Bella Vasquez.

In Vietnam thanks to:
Phan Thuan An.

In Hong Kong thanks to:
Marina Bullivant, Trina Dingler Ebert, Duyen Dang-Hackett & Anthony Hackett, Sandra S.Y. Hu, Yenn Wong.

In China thanks to:
Pallavi Aiyar, Julio Arias, Annie & Roland Marsz, Handel Lee, Tara Wong.

In Japan thanks to:
Saurabh and Bhavna Agnihotri, Tadao Ando and Associates, Hiroshi Araki, Wolfgang J. Angyal, Sandeep Biswas, Azby Brown, John and Asako Duffy, Mark Dytham, David Elliott, Lucy Birmigham Fujii, Amy Hau, Fumi Ikeda, Nirmal Jain, Amy Katoh, Alex Kerr, Kengo Kuma, Aseem R. Mahajan, Peter and Ruksana Massion, Geeta Mehta, Pamela Mori, Biren Nanda, Atul and Hema Parekh, Emiko Fujioka Ogawa, Kazuo Ogawa, Tadashi Ogawa, Tatsuhito Ono, Janak and Rita Raj, Aditya Rana, Keiichi Saiki, Yasuo Satomi, Robert and Yuko Self, Ambassador Aftab Seth and Mrs Pola Seth, Manish Sharma, Edward Suzuki, Amrita Tanabe, Kaoru Tokumasu, Kyoichi Tsuzuki, Alain Wacziarg, Johnnie Walker.

Further thanks go to:
Robert Alderman, Naveen and Raseel Ansal, Aneesha Baig, Daniela Bezzi, Tapas Datta, Yves Demonie, Manvi and Harsh Dhillon, Jane Edwards, Sagarika Ghose, Ashley Hicks, Monica Sue Hoffman (New York), Louis and Gigi de Jonghe, Sonal Joshi, Amitabh Kant, Vikram and Anita Lal, Jane Linklater, Amer Mahmood, Regina Maréchal (Swiss Magazine Basel), Ambassador Philip McDonagh and Ana Grenfell McDonagh, Mike and Kate Metcalf, Lalit and Manjari Nirula, T.N. Ninan, Lekha and Ranjan Poddar, Anupam Poddar, the Poddar Foundation, Peter Popham, Rega (Swiss Air-Rescue), Christiane Reiter, Ravi Sabharwal, Deidi von Schaewen, Sanjeve Sethi, Shalini Sethi, Ajai Shukla, Brijeshwar Singh, Mahijit Singh, Malvika and Tejbir Singh, Prabeen Singh and Arun and Amrita Thapar, Gisela Treichler (Travel Bookshop Zurich), Dudu von Thielmann (Buenos Aires).

Special thanks go to the Indonesia Culture & Tourism Board, the Philippine Convention & Visitors Corporation, the Singapore Tourism Board and to the Japan Foundation for a fellowship that enabled the author to visit Japan in 2003.

The author Sunil Sethi is indebted to Prannoy and Radhika Roy of New Delhi Television for a leave of absence that enabled him to travel in Asia in 2003. He would like to express his special gratitude to his editorial assistant Jayati Sethi, who worked with the utmost diligence.

INDEX

imprint

To stay informed about upcoming TASCHEN titles, please request our magazine at www.taschen.com/magazine
or write to TASCHEN, Hohenzollernring 53, D–50672 Cologne, Germany, contact@taschen.com, Fax: +49-221-254919.
We will be happy to send you a free copy of our magazine which is filled with information about all of our books.

© 2007 TASCHEN GmbH
Hohenzollernring 53
D-50672 Köln
www.taschen.com

CONCEPT, EDITING AND LAYOUT BY
Angelika Taschen, Berlin

DESIGN
Sense/Net, Andy Disl and Birgit Reber, Cologne

GENERAL PROJECT MANAGEMENT
Stephanie Bischoff, Cologne

TEXT COORDINATION AND EDITING
Kirsten E. Lehmann, Cologne

GERMAN TRANSLATION
Anne Brauner, Cologne

FRENCH TRANSLATION
Christèle Jany, Cologne

LITHOGRAPHY MANAGEMENT
Horst Neuzner, Cologne

LITHOGRAPHY
lithotronic media gmbh, Frankfurt am Main

ENDPAPERS
Chinese poster "Acrobatics" by Xu Jiping, 1962
Collection Michael Wolf; www.photomichaelwolf.com

Printed in Italy
ISBN 978-3-8228-4819-7